NotGuilty

DebbieTravis

NotGuilty

My Guide to
Working Hard,
Raising Kids
and Laughing
through the Chaos

RANDOM HOUSE CANADA

Library and Archives Canada Cataloguing in Publication

Travis, Debbie, 1957-
Not guilty : my guide to working hard, raising kids and laughing through
the chaos / Debbie Travis.

ISBN 978-0-307-35722-9

1. Travis, Debbie, 1957-. 2. Travis, Debbie, 1957- –Family.
3. Parenting. 4. Motherhood. 5. Interior decorators–Canada–Biography.
6. Working mothers–Canada–Biography. 7. Television producers and
directors–Canada–Biography. 8. Businesswomen–Canada–Biography.
I. Title.

NK2013.Z9T73 2008   747.092   C2008-904340-5

Printed in the United States of America

2 4 6 8 9 7 5 3 1

*I would like to dedicate this book to our goldfish,
who has never talked back to me, never stayed out late, never
complained about the food and is always
happy to see me.*

Contents

I have absolutely no right to do this book. I am not a child psychologist, a top pediatrician or a marriage counsellor. In fact I don't even have a degree. I left school at sixteen. Even worse, I do not have the answers to being the perfect parent. I should have called the book *The Meltdown* or *Touch Your Brother Again and I'll Rip Your Head Off*.

What I am is a survivor. A working mom. Somehow, I have found the tools to juggle it all, through tears and tantrums (mine not the kids'). So if you have ever wanted to kill a cute little three-year-old, imagined (with delight) your husband disappearing into thin air or dreamed of running over the Grade 5 math teacher, then grab a bottle of wine and this book, run a bath and lock the door. It may save your life.

Why I'm the way I am

"One!"

I'm standing at the bottom of the stairs in my bare feet, hand extended, index finger pointing upward.

"Two!" I'm shouting now. My face is turning raging purple (a colour not unlike Sultry Satin, a favourite in my paint line).

I give Max the Look, the one that every mother perfects over the years. It can stop him and his brother, Josh, in their tracks. Even their father, Hans, doesn't mess with the Look—*You're wearing that shirt? With those pants?*—and he'll turn on his heel like a competitor in *Dancing with the Stars*.

Max glares back, but he can't compete with my nearly twenty years of practice.

Everything was fine a minute ago. The four of us were happily eating a family dinner together. Stories were being batted across the table until the popular subject of how stupid old Mother is with electronics came up again. Yes, it's hilarious, and I don't even mind being the butt of a running joke about how I can no longer turn on the television (with six remotes, it's hard to remember which goes first), but as with any other aspect of family life, there is a fine line. And watch out when that line is crossed! One minute we were all laughing, and the next, Max was talking to me with the foul mouth he usually reserves for one of his mates.

The happy mood turned on a dime. "Don't speak to your mother like that," said Hans (who's usually the easygoing one). "Up to your room. Now!"

I'm still standing at the foot of the stairs. "Two and a half!" I announce. Max comes closer, a sulk transforming his handsome face. I can see the others from where I'm standing, Hans cross that our meal is ruined, Josh pleased with himself, as if his brother's horrid language makes him seem angelic in contrast.

"Honestly, if I have to say . . . thr . . ." Max is now taller than I am and has that gangly teenage-boy walk, leading with his arms. He lumbers by and pats me on the head as if I were the family dog. I can see a tiny grin playing at the corners of his mouth.

"I'm not kidding!" I bellow as my six-foot eighteen-year-old disappears from view. I can hear him slam the bedroom door as I sink onto the stairs. I don't know whether to laugh or cry.

The truth is, I couldn't be happier. Seeing these boys so grown up—and yet still responding to the Look!—I can't help feeling as if I've completed the race, broken through the finish line. I have delivered into this world two young men who are not only all in one piece but well adjusted and happy, nearly ready for families of their own (hopefully not too soon).

Instead of laughing, though, I cry. Great heaving sobs of sadness. Sitting on the lower stair, I can think only that it's all over. My little boys are gone. So are their parents, the ones who were always right, who always knew best. (Well, *they're* still here, but our roles are changing way too fast.)

The tears don't last long. Max peeks over the banister. "Can I come down now? I have a date in an hour," he says, beaming at me.

Meltdowns Are Imperative

When you begin your family, the most irritating comments come from the empty nesters who tell you to enjoy every minute of your time with your children because they grow up so fast. It feels a bit like being taunted when you're racing around working at home, working at work, picking up the dry cleaning, wearing a path in the aisles of the grocery store, trying to maintain some semblance of a marriage, trying to see your friends, ticking off all the boxes on that never-ending to-do list.

The problem is, I'm nearly there, and I've discovered that those empty nesters are absolutely right. Those years when your children are small and dependent on you *do* fly by. There is only one thing I regret, and that's the amount of energy I spent feeling free-floating maternal guilt. What a waste of time.

A few years ago, I was asked to speak to a large group of women at a charity luncheon. It was the first time I'd been asked to talk publicly about something other than decorating. For me, it was incredibly liberating, because although I'm known for my television shows on design, I have also built a thriving television production business, a successful product line and write columns and books—all while trying to be a mum to two active boys and wife to my business partner and very patient husband, Hans.

Like all the women in that audience, I have struggled with the precarious balance of work and family. I didn't think I had anything much to say, no more, really, than any of the other hard-working women there. As I went onstage, the organizer whispered, "Just tell them about your life."

So I did. I told them how I'd started from nothing, moving to Canada from England after I met Hans, building up a decorative-painting business while my kids were small, then turning that into *The Painted House*, a hit show that ran for thirteen seasons and sold in over eighty countries. I talked about how watching other families when I was painting in their homes and later filming the TV shows, I had a bird's-eye view into the dynamics of parents and children, husbands and wives.

I told the women there how watching these other families made me think about my own kids and about the stories we all have to tell—some ridiculous, others sad, many, many that are hilarious. Seeing all that drama, and the way families act under pressure, gave me the germ of the idea for our award-winning show *Facelift*, the first-ever reality program on home decorating, in which one person in a family is given a surprise home makeover by our team.

I explained that all this showed me how normal it is to have meltdowns. It's perfectly common to swing wildly between loving our husbands and children and wanting to throw them out the window. Contrary to popular thinking these days, most mothers aren't wearing stilettos in the grocery store, and it's absolutely natural to have spit-up dripping down your back and to think nothing of carrying around a purse with a full diaper in it. I was amazed that they seemed to be hanging on my every word.

When I finished, there was some time left for questions. One woman stood up and went over to the microphone. She said she owned two coffee-shop franchises and was the mother of three children. "My question to you, Debbie, is, how do you get up in the morning?" She promptly burst into tears and then, to my horror, everyone in the audience began to cry.

It was an incredibly cathartic experience for the people there—including me—but also an indication of how stressed out and fearful so many women are these days. They feel guilty about even the smallest things. Is the world really going to implode if you don't bake cookies for the school bake sale or if little Johnny has holes in his shoes because you haven't had time to go shopping? Does it matter if your house is spotless for the mothers' group? Women are obsessing about every little thing their children do and thinking they have to be these glossy packages all the time— skinny and gorgeous, successful at work, with charming compliant children at home. The women at that talk were just relieved that someone was saying they didn't have to be perfect, that we all make mistakes, and it's all right not only to cry but to laugh at the insanity that is motherhood.

A Little Humiliation Goes a Long Way

Women of my mother's generation can teach us all a lot. Their world and their lives were very different from our own, of course, but they had an attitude that's worth remembering. They didn't go around feeling guilty about their kids all the time; they just seemed to get on with things. (My mum certainly wasn't finishing my homework at midnight or marching into the school to take my side against a teacher about my rotten behaviour!) The mothers I grew up surrounded by in the north of England spent time with their friends, didn't cling to their children and had an innate ability to laugh at their own misfortune.

I was born and raised in Lancashire, a county in the northwest of England. It's a hardy place that has produced tough farmers and millworkers whose survival is thanks to the pub (there's one on nearly every street) and their legendary sense of humour. My parents fitted the mould perfectly.

My father's family owned a factory that manufactured candy machines for the famous sweet companies Cadbury, Rowntree and Mars. My claim to fame has always been that my great-grandfather invented the Gummi Bear. (Now, that puts you top of the heap at show and tell!) My dad was an engineer, and he worked for the family company. You couldn't have a better father. He was a quiet, gentle man who adored his wife and children—three girls (of which I'm the eldest) and one boy.

The highlight of my younger years was to visit him at the candy factory—and have him all to myself. It was this great old Victorian mill straight out of *Charlie and the Chocolate Factory*. The ground floor was the size of a football pitch and filled with enormous machines being tested for the manufacture of new sweets. My favourite was the Gobstopper machine. He would boost me up so I could lean over and look into the huge vat to watch the Gobstoppers (the equivalent of blackballs in North America) being made. I loved to see the little aniseeds spinning around and around, then the dye and candy coating them, then another colour and another until there was a solid ball of hard candy. It was just the right size to choke a child and, in fact, did choke many children (there have been calls to ban them ever since, but there can be little joy more pure than sucking that gigantic ball of colour until it's a seed once again!).

There were also oversized tracks on the ceiling from which hung hooks so large that a small child could sit in them. My father would lift me up there, press a button and I'd swing high over the bubbling vats of boiling sugar. I was warned never to tell my mother, since she would no doubt have killed him. It was thrilling not only to ride the hooks but to have shared this secret with him and have a chance to be alone with my dad.

He really was the perfect father. He could build anything. We didn't just have a rabbit cage for our rabbits, but he built a huge run with alleys and tunnels where they could race about. He even built us our own trampoline, swings and a slide.

On my eighth birthday, I was worried when there was no big present waiting for me in the house. But just when I was about to despair, a dusty truck drove into our small driveway. My father dragged me by the hand to watch as the dump truck reared up outside our front door and a ton of bricks tumbled out. That was my birthday present—the best ever. I built every configuration of playhouse that summer. Other kids had a Wendy house, as we called it, in their backyard, but I had a new one every day. The bricks just needed a good shove to come tumbling down (usually with snot-faced Jimmy from next door inside), and I'd just build a new structure again. Thirty years later I gave each of my boys a fat length of rope for Christmas. That rope was used in every game and adventure: I think it's the best present they ever received and certainly the one they always remember.

My father was wonderful, but it was my mother who ruled the roost. All the mothers did where I grew up. They would gather at their back fences, sharing stories, laughing and complaining. It was the thing that saved them from their hard lives.

My mum was loud and funny and had loads of friends. She was also busy all the time, running around with a kid on one hip and an iron in the other hand. We were fairly middle class compared with the rest of our village, and my parents actually built their own home—a rarity then. And when I say "built" I mean that my mother carried the bricks and my father laid them.

Money was tight, but we hardly noticed. I got the new clothes, being the eldest, and my sisters got my hand-me-downs. Errands and chores were essential, and they were to be completed with a smile on your face. Vacuuming the house was my responsibility—not a small task considering we had carpet everywhere, including in the loo and kitchen—Brits just love their carpet! Punishment was not being allowed to play outside with your friends. We wouldn't have cared a bit if television was taken away since there was little to watch and we'd far rather have been up a tree.

Humiliation was a large part of growing up in those days in the U.K. It's a complete no-no today, but I think a good dose of firmness around what is acceptable and what is not is a must. There are two kinds of humiliation: the bad kind, when parents or teachers are bullies, making a child feel small and powerless, but the other type—when it's about teaching something that will help them in life—shows children humility rather than shame. It gives them tools for their future.

My first real foray into being hideously humiliated by my mum was when I was about eight years old. In many of the corner stores in our village there was a lifesize ceramic statue of a sad-looking boy in leg braces—known as the Cripple in those politically incorrect times. There was a slot on his head for dropping coins in for a polio charity, as Britain had emerged from the epidemic only a decade before. Mr. Patel, who ran the shop, was a huge man—or so he seemed to us at the time—and he also had a glass eye. We were mesmerized by this and especially loved the fact that he had a blind spot: great for pinching candies.

The best part was that the statue had a broken piece at the back of the foot that had been Scotch-taped up, and if we were quick enough and quiet enough we could pull off the tape, get our hands in and grab a fistful of coins before Mr. Patel spotted us. My best friend and I had perfected the art of finding the perfect angle and the right moment when his blind spot and the magazine rack hid us from view. We thought ourselves incredibly clever stealing from the charity Cripple several weeks in a row.

But our weekend nicking came to a crashing halt when we were finally caught—not by the gentle Mr. Patel but by my mother. She had a way of entering a room without a sound and quietly standing over you until you jumped out of your skin when you realized she was there. It was a rainy Saturday afternoon, and my friend and I were happily counting our loot on the floor of my bedroom when she walked in, using her stealth move. It didn't take much interrogation from her to find out where the fortune had come from.

My mother sent my friend home, and with the coins in a paper bag, she frog-marched me back to the store to confess my crime to Mr. Patel. She had me not only return the money but also wash his store windows for the next four weekends. It was humiliating, sure, traumatizing, yes, but I never stole again.

My mother was a real Northerner, a no-nonsense type of woman. We weren't given choices at dinnertime—or tea, as it was known. (There was none of this asking each member of the family what they'd like to eat, as I have found myself doing more than once.) It was a boiled egg at 4 p.m., thank you very much.

All my life, I've endured jokes about British cooking, and while things have changed a wee bit with Jamie Oliver and other celebrity chefs, during my childhood meals were bland and plain. Green beans were put on to boil until they practically disintegrated, and the roast beef was cooked until it tasted and looked like leather. It's an English tradition to have a roast for Sunday lunch, and my mother had a talent for making the remains last another five meals. We ate various types of "spot the meat" stews most of the week.

As immigrants poured into England over the late 1950s and '60s, tastes began to change (chicken masala is now England's national dish). As we sat around the kitchen table one evening my mother made a shocking announcement: "I want you to brace yourselves: we're having foreign food tonight." We gasped—me with excitement, the younger ones in horror—as she presented us with bowls of Heinz tinned spaghetti. We'd never seen pasta before, and we were amazed.

It was an idyllic childhood. But then my father was diagnosed with colon cancer. He had many, many surgeries and became excruciatingly thin. He had loads of scars, so many that we could play checkers on his stomach. We knew he was ill, but we had busy lives of our own, playing with friends, going to school and Brownies, and we didn't think about it much.

Amazingly, my baby brother, William, was born in that time (I'm not sure how they did it—it must have been immaculate conception). Years later, my mother told me that they'd both desperately wanted a son. But my sisters, Joanna and Emma, and I couldn't have cared less. We were furious. We had planned for a girl, and her name was to be Helen. In fact, we called my brother Helen for the first two years of his life. (I can't even count the clips behind the ears that we all received for our stubbornness!)

The day Will was born was a wild one. My headmistress poked her head around the classroom door to tell me my mother was waiting outside. I was furious to be missing gym class, and I glared at her as she sped off at top speed for the hospital that had once been a Victorian workhouse and remained dank and dingy still. "I am about to have this baby, and I need you to carry my things," she said.

I sat with her in that dismal room as she ran around,

jumping over the bed again and again. "I need to have this baby this afternoon," she told me. "I have to get back to your dad."

She gave birth while I finished my homework in the waiting room, and several hours later we were back in the car, headed home, with me holding the new bundle in the rear seat.

My mother didn't tell us much about Dad's illness, but my sisters and I knew something was odd when he was at home while other fathers were off working. Then as he became more and more sick, he was in his dressing gown all the time. I know he tried to get dressed so he wouldn't look so ill when we returned from school. Parents try to hide so much from their children, forgetting from their own childhoods that kids don't miss a beat.

The day my dad died is as clear to me as if it happened yesterday. Billy, as my father was known to everyone, had been sent home from the hospital with no hope of getting better. I have a letter he wrote to his sister a few weeks earlier when he was still at St. George's, a famous cancer hospital in London. In it, he describes the chemotherapy—a new treatment at the time. They dropped the raw chemicals straight into his colon, he said, and it was like being burned from the inside out. He felt that it would be better if he just came home and said goodbye to his family.

At the time, of course, I was aware of little of this. What I knew was that memorable weekend I'd been sent off for a sleepover at my friend's house. It was a big deal because staying over with friends was not common in those days. We had all kinds of plans, but in the morning my friend's mother came in and said, "You have to go home now."

Cross at having my weekend ruined, I drove with her parents back to my home. As we turned off the main road and up the avenue to our house, I noticed that all the curtains were drawn. Why is nobody awake? I wondered. I'd had knots in my stomach before taking tests at school, but they were butterflies; this felt more like a fat fist.

My grandmother, my mother's mother, answered the door. She was my idol, a wildly vivacious woman who lived in the south of France, owned antique shops and had married several bankers. She was glamorous and chic—quite unlike anyone else I knew.

She looked at me and said, "You better go upstairs and wait in your room."

The doorbell kept ringing, people going in and out, until the house was finally silent. My mother must have been waiting until all the children were home to tell us together. It was awful.

She was thirty-three years old. He had been only thirty-nine. Mum was now a widow with four children, the youngest just six months old. She made us all sleep in her bed that night. His death hadn't really sunk in. All I remember is the bickering and fidgeting as we squished together.

Even when something tragic happens in a family, there is always going to be a reality check. There is no other option—life just goes on.

Steal the Housekeeping

I don't remember my mother ever saying "I love you" to me. She probably did, but she had a big dose of that old British reserve: it was more of a pat on the back as I headed for London after a weekend at home. How that has changed! One of the most wonderful aspects of my children's generation is their lack of self-consciousness about expressing their feelings. My boys don't think twice about shouting, "Bye! Love you, Mum," as they race out the door with their friends—it's something I've been saying to them daily all their lives.

But my mother's reserve is something she came by honestly. She was sent away to boarding school at seven, an age when most of us are still totally dependent on family life. Still, it was common practice at the time.

My grandmother (who was definitely living in the wrong era) worked hard campaigning for politicians and city councils. She was always beautifully dressed, and in the scrapbook of newspaper clippings I have of her, she stands out in a sea of matronly bosoms and sensible shoes. She looks so elegant in her tight pencil skirts, a fox throw draping her shoulders. She was not a "mummy" type at all.

Even when my mum would come home for the school holidays when she was a child, she had to fend for herself. She biked thirty miles across the hills just to get there. She adored her mother, but vied for her attention with Granny's many other interests and commitments. Mum didn't talk much about her childhood—probably since most of it was spent at school—but she did tell me about the day when she was eleven and came home for the long Easter weekend. Halfway through their evening meal, Granny announced, "Oh! I knew there was something I forgot to tell you. Your father died two months ago. Would you like pudding, dear?" My mother never really got over it—but you have to laugh, they were such a different generation.

We've swung so far in the opposite direction that parents now imagine they have to be cool and trendy, part of their kids' pack of friends. We tell our kids everything. But it's a fine line to walk—and very similar to the delicate relationship between employer and employee.

Working on our television shows is demanding, but we also have a lot of fun during the crazy, intense days of filming. The crew will often head out for a drink together, and while I love being part of the team, I know there is a time when the boss has to step away. Get too familiar and it comes back to bite you in the bum! It's the same with family. Sharing stories with your teenagers of getting stoned or having sex is guaranteed to come back and haunt you.

There has to be a place between the formality of my childhood and the over-closeness of today. I think creating a slight fear factor with your children, a kind of distance, can actually make things run more smoothly, especially when they're young. Children crave knowing what the family's boundaries are and how they need to behave within them. They want to know what the rules are.

After my dad died, it was clear I had to grow up really fast. Over the years, I've met many kids who have lost a parent at the age I did. Twelve is a hard time—you're not a child anymore, but you're not an adult, either.

I knew we were pretty broke after he died. The candy factory had gone bankrupt years before, and to add insult to injury, death duties were phenomenally high at the time. The bailiff arrived five days after my father's death to claim everything. But my mother was smart. She'd already taken all their savings out of their joint account and lifted the antiques my grandmother had given her over the fence to be stored in a neighbour's shed. When the bailiff turned up, the house had nothing of value left for those low-lifes to haul away.

Watching my mother take control only a few days after being widowed was one of the key events in my life. Seeing her strength during that time was a real lesson in survival. It made me realize that every woman, whatever her age or income, needs to have some backdoor money. You might put a little aside from your paycheque each week or "steal" a bit of the housekeeping money—it doesn't really matter—but we all need to have something socked away so that if, for whatever reason, you're desperate to leave, you can grab the kids or pay the rent or whatever it takes to make it through.

I don't remember the lack of money being a huge obstacle in our lives, though after my dad died my sisters were pulled out of the private school we all went to. They were just starting and I was already well along. God knows what my mother said (or did) to the headmaster, but she went in to see him and came out twenty minutes later and told me I was going to be there until I turned sixteen. "Behave!" she said with the standard clip on the ear.

My mother was still so young, and she was very lonely. She was an attractive woman, but she was always home in the evenings. She was probably seen as a threat in our small village—an eligible widow. I have no idea if she ever dreamed of having a career. In those days in Lancashire, the only women who worked were in a factory, a shop or scrubbing someone else's floor. There was little chance of a career—I'm not sure if the word even existed for them.

Two years after my father's death, Mum met and married her second husband. Life changed for all of us. My stepfather, John Travis, fitted in well with his new young family—except for me. I became an unpleasant teenager. I couldn't wait to start out on my own. I left school at sixteen. Even my career counsellor thought I was a lost cause. "Well, you're never going to be a nurse. A secretary? I don't think so. And I doubt anyone will marry you. I really don't know what you're going to do," he said, hustling me out the door.

Blow Your Own Horn

"All you have is your looks; you're not very bright," was my grandmother's constant refrain. My mother, on the other hand, told me, "You'll never be a great beauty, so it's your clever brain you have to rely on." With that type of self-esteem building I should have been in a psych ward the rest of my life!

They weren't being intentionally cruel—still, I can't imagine ever being quite so brutal with my own kids. It did stop you from becoming big-headed. It also made me more determined. I decided I didn't really care what they thought. I headed for the big-city lights and landed in London at the tender age of seventeen.

I had started modelling a few months earlier, when I met a man during a long bus ride. He asked me to get off the bus with him in the middle of nowhere so he could take my picture. I was so naïve. I said, "Yeah, all right," and we hopped off at the next stop. He took me out into a field and posed me beside a tree. Then we hopped right back on the bus. (What I would do to my kids if they ever did anything quite so stupid would probably have me in jail!) Two days later, my picture turned up in the local paper beside an article called "Today's Youth." A modelling agency saw it, called me up and before you could say *fish and chips* I was headed to their sister agency in Milan. My parents where far from pleased, but it wasn't long before I'd built up a portfolio of photographs.

Within weeks of moving to London, I was shipped off again, this time to Tokyo. That's where I really learned my stuff. I worked every day for six months. I think I talked to my mother twice. She'd write me these elaborate, long letters saying, "Your brother Will saw a bird today," and there

I was seeing all these mind-blowing places, learning so much. My family had barely been out of the north of England. Where I come from, if you marry someone in the next village you're considered really out there, and there I was living in Japan.

When I returned home, I felt so far from that little village. Not that I was blowing my own trumpet. I wasn't allowed. Once, I did a hat campaign for the department store Marks & Spencer. I told my mother about it, said my picture was on all these big billboards, that I was the Marks hat girl. She said, "That's nice, love," and carried on speaking to somebody. She wasn't going to have me showing off. Two days later, though, she hired a bus and took all her friends to the store in Manchester so they could walk around and see the pictures.

I know my mother was proud of me, but it wasn't something she went around bragging about. I actually think that lingering Northern reluctance to sing your own praises is what's kept me so grounded over the years.

After Japan, I was a seasoned professional model. I had a base in London but I travelled all over Europe. It is probably the most boring job in the world. I always talk about passion and finding something you love to do as a career, but sometimes, especially when you're young, you just don't know. Watching my own children figure out what they are passionate about, I see again how scary and frustrating it can be.

But for me, it arrived in a flash. I was working on a television commercial in Holland, sitting around waiting to be called to do my bit. The action on the set was fascinating, and my eyes were drawn to an older woman (she must have been all of twenty-seven) who held a yellow clipboard. Her arms were a constant flurry of pointing and gesturing: "You! Over there! Get that model to stand straight!" I felt it in my heart: I wanted a clipboard. Badly. I also wanted to do something more creative than putting on dresses and smiling for the camera. When I arrived back in London I began to work my way into the television world.

I had begun to assist on various shows when my mother developed colon cancer. She had such a good sense of humour that even during chemotherapy she was making light of things. She told me one story about how she and her husband were leaving the hospital following her treatment and all of a sudden he starts tearing off his clothes and running all over the car park. She was weak and could barely walk after the chemo, and there she is watching this very straitlaced man she's married to acting like some crazed maniac. Turns out a bee had flown up his pant leg and stung him on the scrotum. She laughed and laughed. She could make even the worst turn of events sound funny.

I never loved her as much as I did the very last time I saw her. She was just fifty-four but had been sick for nearly seven years by then. I hadn't realized how ill she was. She certainly wouldn't have told me, and my stepfather didn't want to alarm us. I was about four months pregnant with her first grandchild, and I'd travelled back to the U.K. to stay with her. She came to see me off at the train station and said goodbye on the platform. I watched her through the window as she waved when my train pulled away. I saw her mouth the words "I love you."

Mother Knows Best

When we're young, we all vow not to become like our mothers. I remember my mum embarrassed me so much when I was a teenager that I wouldn't even walk on the same side of the street. I would cringe when she screamed from the bottom of the stairs at me and my sisters. I despised her rage and empty threats—she did *not* have a suitcase packed for a tropical beach where they banned children. I thought that when I became a mother I would talk to my children with dignity, treat them like equals!

Of course, now I see her in my mind when I'm counting one, two, three for my eighteen-year-old, or when I look up from my desk and notice the card Max made me for Valentine's Day when he was a boy. "If I could fly, I'd fly you to England, I'd fly you to your old house," it reads—for that was *my* threat whenever the boys were driving *me* mad.

It's hard to believe when you're functioning so well in the outside world, building a company or running a business or performing surgery, that at home you turn into this nagging fishwife. Motherhood is such a complicated mass of mixed feelings. It is the best of times and the worst of times. It can produce such highs of happiness and joy, and such deep anger that you can hardly believe it came out of you. One minute you are this vivacious, lively woman, and the next you are your mother.

When the boys were nine or ten and home with a babysitter, I came in the door to peals of laughter ringing through the house. I have never switched so fast from being happy to blood-curdlingly furious. We had bought them two miniature rabbits as an Easter gift instead of buckets of chocolate, and they were standing at the top of the stairs sliding the rabbits down in frying pans as if the stairs were a toboggan run. They'd stacked pillows at the end for a soft landing but those rabbits were practically airborne, their little ears pinned back against their heads.

"What the hell are you doing?" I screamed.

"Mom, they're happy, look at their little mouths."

"That's not a smile, it's gravity!"

I was beside myself. "You'll never have another pet!" I picked up the rabbits and stormed off, putting them in a laundry basket outside on the deck while I tried to figure out what to do with the boys. Within five minutes, some raccoons had eaten them.

When the boys saw the hair all over the deck they both burst into tears. "You killed our rabbits!"

"No, they've left home with their suitcases," I said, scrambling to gain the upper hand. "They've gone on holiday from you two."

I called Hans and told him he had to come home right away. I couldn't deal with it. I was going home to England!

"Let me get this straight," he said, "You took their little bunnies off them and fed them to a raccoon?"

"No! I put them on the deck and they were eaten."

"Muuuuum, you said they went on holiday."

"Hans," I pleaded. "They put them in a frying pan."

"They were cooking them?"

"No, they put the rabbits on a toboggan run."

"But there's no snow," he said.

"It doesn't matter, Hans!" I screamed. "I'm right! I'm their mother." The kids were staring at me as I shouted into the phone, stamping my foot. "I. Am. Their. Mother!!"

I should have said, for better or for worse.

All the baby books will tell you that pregnancy is the most wonderful time in your life. What they don't tell you is that it's the beginning of the end of being a self-absorbed glamourpuss. You see those mums pushing million-dollar strollers, wearing designer outfits and towering heels and think they've got it all. But look closely, and you'll see the grubby handprint at the back of their skirt, or the uneven part of their hair where they've just cut out gum that was rubbed in while they tried to leave the house. I know there are some women who pull off the supermum beautifully, but they surely aren't happy, and I'm certain their kids will turn out to be serial killers.

This lack of pride in one's appearance creeps up on you slowly through your pregnancy. You go from gorgeous expectant mum with a little bump to "You look truly glowing" at six months to "Oh dear, did you have acne before?" to "You know there is surgery for those thighs" at the end. And if you still feel in charge of your looks at nine months, the birth will be certain to put you right. Any remaining vanity flies right out the window when the pushing begins. Your partner's adoring gaze over candlelight and chardonnay is replaced by a look of shock at the bottom of the hospital bed—"I think I'll stand over here for a bit," he says, eyes wide with horror. A month later you'll be chatting quite normally to friends about your hemorrhoids and the different solutions for cracked nipples. Yes, life has changed forever.

2

Frilly little thongs and big puffy bottoms

There is nothing more mind-numbingly boring than other women telling their stories of giving birth in minute-by-minute detail. Mine, on the other hand, is riveting. First of all, the man in the birthing room with me was a relative stranger. I hadn't even known him a year. I'd probably only been on ten dates with him as a singleton, and there I was, the size of a small cruise ship, swearing at his panicked face in language that would put a dockworker to shame.

I had first set eyes on Hans a year earlier at a fancy party at the Cannes Film Festival in the south of France. He's German but was living in Canada, and was there buying film distribution rights. He is probably the most un-German-looking bloke on the planet, with his thick wavy black hair, almond-shaped green eyes and an adorable grin that had me acting with the morals of a sewer (as my mother would have said). I had my own tiny production company in London and was trying to sell a documentary I'd just started to produce about self-made millionaires. But the project was ditched, as was life as I'd known it. From that night on, we were glued at the hip, and within a few weeks we were married. With rose-coloured glasses and the excitement of a war bride, I followed him across the Atlantic to his one-bedroom apartment in Montreal.

It was only a couple of months after we married that we had to return to Europe on business. We stayed at the Dolder Grand in Zurich, the banking capital of Switzerland. It was incredibly posh. Most of the hotels I'd stayed in before were just scruffy rooms shared with a bunch of girls on holidays. I don't think I'd ever seen a duvet before, or that room service card they leave you in expensive hotels to check off what you'd like served in the morning. I was so excited and impressed that I sat down and filled in the breakfast card really carefully, studying it as if it was an exam. I even put my name and address on it. I checked off that I'd like a boiled egg with toast and tea.

In the morning I was so looking forward to my breakfast that the first thing I did when I woke up was say to Hans, "So, where's my egg?" He told me he didn't bother putting out the card because we were in a rush to leave. (He was probably running from the bill!) Well, I cried all the way from Zurich to Milan. All I talked about was that boiled egg. All I wanted was just a little egg, was it too much to ask for, and on and on. With gritted teeth he sped down the autostrada, no doubt wondering what kind of nagging maniac he'd married. I kept up the rant for what must have been the longest eight-hour drive the poor man had ever endured.

That night we had dinner at a bustling restaurant in Milan with a bunch of television people. We were sitting there having our drinks when suddenly a whole line of waiters appeared, the last one carrying a gigantic silver service in his raised hand. He put the tray down in front of me as if I were the Queen herself. In the middle of a plate of lettuce was this perfectly boiled egg. I knew I'd married the right guy, as he beamed his now-familiar grin at me. But the next morning, I realized something was up. I just didn't feel right, and my crazy behaviour the previous day was actually unusual for me. I crept out of the hotel to the pharmacy to get a pregnancy test. I was pregnant–in Italian.

I loved every minute of those nine months. Mostly because I could eat anything. For eight years when I was modelling, I simply didn't eat. I was determined to catch up on all the food I'd missed, and because I couldn't find any TV work, I just stayed home, watched the soaps and stuffed my face. I would sit there surrounded by tubs of creamy yogurt and ham sandwiches, weeping at some wild story about someone's twin brother's amnesia. The guilt I felt had nothing to do with how much I ate, it was that I was having the laziest time of my life and Hans was off working hard to keep me in food! I actually kept a bucket of water and some rubber gloves nearby so if he came home unexpectedly I could pretend I'd just been scrubbing the floor like any good housewife.

It was strange to go from what was quite a glamorous life—I had my own apartment on the King's Road in London and thought nothing of jetting off to the south of France for the weekend—to being this enormous but very happy hippo. Hans must have wondered what he'd got into. He'd married an ex-model who could barely go out for dinner without checking herself out in the mirror forty times, and suddenly there I was with feet so swollen that I couldn't even wear shoes. I got so fat that it looked as if my neck had fused with my torso.

The doctor stopped weighing me when I'd gained eighty pounds. Doctors today say twenty-five pounds is recommended for the average woman. Give me a break—I put that on each thigh! After a while I could only fit in this one drop-waist denim dress. (Years later, the kids found it and turned it into a teepee in the backyard.) I looked like an old washerwoman, waddling along, my great big puffy bottom swaying from side to side.

After a while my doctor figured out that I had gestational diabetes, which accounted for some of the weight gain—the rest was thanks to my hourly snacks. I had to go into the hospital regularly and be monitored. One day the specialist took me aside and asked to speak to me privately.

My heart sank. Pictures of four-headed babies and the chimp child in the *Guinness World Records* flooded through my mind. The chair creaked beneath my weight, but I was too scared to be embarrassed.

"It's about your underwear, dear," she said kindly. "Do you really need to wear that tiny, frilly little thong?"

"But they told us in prenatal classes to still make an effort to look sexy for our husbands," I sputtered.

"Yes, dear, but they're cutting off the circulation in your legs."

The day Josh was born was the hottest of that entire year. My legs were stuck together from thighs to ankles—not a pretty sight—making it even harder than usual to waddle. The doctor had agreed to induce me, and we were ready to rock and roll. Hans insisted on filming the whole day, but since video cameras in those days were the size of a small shed, I had to carry all the bags as he followed behind me with the bloody thing perched on his shoulder. You can see me in the home movie schlepping bags up the steep hospital driveway wearing that demin dress, my big bottom stealing the scene.

But the filming came to an abrupt end not long after we got to the hospital, and just as my agony was reaching its height. The last frame of the video is a hideous shot of me grabbing in the direction of Hans's throat after you've heard his cheerful comment, "Come on now, give us a smile. It can't hurt that much!" Then "Aaahhhhggg!" and a big bang as the camera hit the floor.

But even without that beautiful moment captured on tape for all eternity, our filming wouldn't have gone on much longer. Hans hates—and I mean truly, madly loathes—needles, the sight of blood and anything that even slightly resembles a chicken (having witnessed their slaughter in German butcher shops when he was a child, he can't even be in the same neighbourhood as one—dead or alive). As the quite gorgeous South African anesthetist waved the epidural needle around, a second thump resounded in the birthing room. Hans hit the floor, and everyone's attention was on him. I lost all hope of ever having a date with the hot anesthetist (a girl has to dream—even when she is rolled on her side like a beached whale with her bum exposed to the world). The nurses transferred me to a chair so they could put my husband on the bed. He actually had to have an IV drip. They couldn't move him. I was more comfortable on the chair, anyway, and two hours later, that's where I had my first son.

There is a raging debate going on in hospitals these days about the wisdom of having fathers in the birthing room. The nurses say it was easier in the old days when they stayed outside, pacing in the corridor. I have to agree.

Josh's birth, however, was nothing compared with the birth of son number two. That time, though, it had nothing to do with the actual labour. I'm jumping ahead in the timeline here, but I can never resist the opportunity to tell a good story.

It was a year later, and I was once again the size of a house, and just about at my due date. Hans and I were hosting a hugely important Hollywood director and his small entourage. It was Sunday morning, and Josh was with a babysitter while we took the group to a famous breakfast place. They were worried about getting on their flight back to Los Angeles later that morning, but the city was quiet and we were confident that we could get them there on time. There was even parking—usually impossible—and the lineup that generally snakes down the street outside the restaurant was missing. The place, in fact, was virtually empty.

We had breakfast, talked business, and everyone was happy. Then, at around ten-thirty, we headed for the car and realized that while we'd been eating, the streets had been entirely roped off. Barricades were everywhere. The smiles on the faces of the director and his entourage melted. "We have to catch our flight!"

Hans reversed down the street at breakneck speed, only to find another barricade and police everywhere. We tried a side street, but discovered that there was no access to the main road toward the airport. We were sitting there trying to figure out what to do, when suddenly cyclists appeared out of nowhere, sprinting by us. We were smack in the middle of the city's annual bike race. A cop poked his head through the car window and told us to be patient; we would have to wait at least an hour for all the competitors to pass by. Our guests would definitely miss their flight. They were not pleased.

Hans tried to back up again, hoping to find another way out of the maze, but that's when my genius, befuddled, highly pregnant brain kicked into gear. "Stop!" I screamed. "Leave it to me!"

I leapt—or more likely lumbered—out of the Jeep and headed for the barrier where a group of determined-looking police officers were standing. With acting worthy of an Oscar, I went into labour standing on the side of the road while bikes whizzed past. Meg Ryan's orgasm scene in *When Harry Met Sally* has nothing on my performance.

I had figured they'd simply stop the race for a minute and let us drive through to get to the "hospital," but those concerned cops had a better idea. They called the ambulance that was waiting around the corner in case there were any bike accidents and threw in a four-bike motorcade to escort us. I sheepishly climbed in, but Hans was not amused. "You can find your own way home once they drop you at emergency," he hissed in my ear. "We're going to get a massive bill from the city for this!"

True to his word, Hans didn't come to get me right away. But after being guided into the hospital by the sweetest policemen ever, I told the hospital staff my story and got them and myself laughing so hard that my water broke. Hans, of course, turned up when he realized I was no longer crying wolf, and seven hours later our second child, Max, arrived. (We never did receive a bill for the ambulance, and the Americans caught the next flight to L.A.—sometimes there is a happy ending!)

Isn't He Lovely?

There is nothing in the world like those early few weeks at home with your first baby. Family, friends, neighbours and colleagues treat you like the queen you are. Sure, you're exhausted, but the constant oohing and aahing and, of course, the prezzies get you through. But take it from me, if you hit another home run within the next year or so, all that lovely attention slows to a trickle.

The first New Year's Eve after Josh's birth we went back to London. It was one of the first parties I'd been to since becoming a mum, and I planned to have a brilliant time downing buckets of champagne. I was dressed in a way-too-tight dress that bordered on offensive, but I really didn't care; I was just proud that I'd already lost fifty pounds of that pregnancy blubber (even though *I* knew it was all water).

Hurtling off the dance floor when I saw the first bottle of champagne arrive at our table, I didn't even wait for the toast. "Yum!" I squealed after the first sip. But that momentary pleasure was followed by a deep sense of dread. It tasted horrid, rather like perfume—the same as it had when I was pregnant with Josh. I said nothing that evening, but the next morning I trotted off on that oh-so-familiar journey to the pharmacist. This time the test was in English, but the results were the same. A few days later, I took Hans out for a supposedly romantic dinner.

"So, do you like having a baby?" I asked him, as we sat in this cozy restaurant.

"Yeah, it's great," he said.

"Do you want another?"

"Sure, maybe in a few years," he said.

"How about eight months?"

We just sat there stunned. Married, two kids and living in a new country—all in just over a year. It was a wee bit overwhelming.

I don't know how many couples plan their families with precision, or how many leave it to chance, but I do know from experience that if you have the remotest idea you'd like to pace your kids a few years apart, do not listen to the old wives' tale about breastfeeding as birth control. It certainly didn't work for me!

With one child, it's easy to imagine you might be able to maintain your fabulous single lifestyle. For the first year after Josh was born, we simply strapped him on our backs and carried on as if our lives were the same. We took him to restaurants and put his basket under the table—he was no more trouble than a small dog. Friends invited us to dinner parties, and we let him sleep on their bed. We even travelled the world. But with two kids, you're suddenly not quite as welcome at those parties and visits with friends. You don't even want to travel the world.

And it's not just other people—if they're honest, most mums will admit to being a wee bit giddier about the birth of their first baby. It's a bit like the first time you visit your favourite city. It's breathtaking and wondrous. You think you'll never get enough. The next time you go, you find it's still wonderful, but the magic has dimmed a little. Having babies is similar. It doesn't mean you love your second (or third or fourth) child any less—in fact, it's often easier to enjoy them because some of the fear has gone and you're just getting on with the job.

The baby scrapbooks where parents record their children's growth, their best handwriting and tufts of hair probably tell the story best. As I'm the eldest of four, my baby book is filled in from the first page to the last. My first smile, first gurgle and first word are all recorded for posterity. Mum diligently wrote in the date when I walked, smiled and even pooed the first time. For my second sister, Joanna, Mum hastily scribbled in the first two pages; for Emma, she noted her name and gave up. My brother, Will, well, he doesn't even have a baby book.

When Josh was born I looked around at the other newborns in the hospital and pitied their parents. He was beautiful, and their children just seemed plain in comparison. I felt superior. I had produced this young god—a masterpiece. Now when I look back at the pictures, I wonder what kind of hormone pumps through a new mum's body to make us thrill at the sight of our own offspring.

The second day after Josh's birth—this was in the years when you weren't whipped out of the hospital before the stitches were finished—one of the nurses told me that my baby had been chosen as the model for the diapering demonstration. I was so proud, she might as well have announced that he had just been accepted by Harvard. To the horror of the head nurse, I invited a small crowd of friends and relatives to witness his stage debut. She was lucky I hadn't called in the local press!

Josh was the happiest baby. There is no doubt in my mind that infants sense your state of mind and act accordingly. When my brother was a baby he cried continuously. It was as if he felt Mum's deep sadness about my father's death in his little bones.

We didn't have the space to give Will a room of his own, so my mother and I adapted a smelly old upstairs loo. Together we ripped out the rotting carpet, washed the floors and applied a fresh coat of paint (little did I realize it would be practice for things to come!). We tucked his bed in there, leaving just enough room for a person to slide between the wall and the bars of the crib. My room was right next door, and I listened from under my sheets when he wailed night after night. Mum would go in and grip the bars of the crib and shake it so much that I thought he would die. "Please stop, please stop," she would sob. I soon learned to leap up at the baby's first whimper and bundle him into bed with me. I did this for the next few years, giving her a chance to sleep, and Will and I an opportunity to form a friendship that would last a lifetime.

With Josh, I was in the honeymoon phase of motherhood. He would wake up every morning blissfully content. He had so much fat on his face that you could barely see his eyes. He looked like a little round Buddha. He would just lie there with a grin. After the first blush of happiness at this state of affairs, I started to wonder if it was normal, if Josh was not quite right in the head.

I took him to our pediatrician and burst into tears. "I think there's something wrong with him. He's so big and he never cries. He just sits there and smiles all the time."

The doctor looked at Josh and he looked at me. "There's nothing wrong with your baby," he said, ushering me out of the office. "He's just fat."

Sometimes doctors and nurses have no idea how frightened young mothers can be. You're dealing with the biggest event in your life, and you're terrified of doing something wrong. It's a very scary time, and you start to worry about the most ridiculous things. Of course, at the time it doesn't feel silly as you leaf frantically through every possible parenting book, looking for the answers.

I recently spoke to a young mother whose eight-week-old daughter was going in for her first inoculation. She hadn't slept for days just thinking about her little baby crying from the needle. She was fretting about whether she should dose her with Tylenol or sugar water and if so, exactly how much she would use. I told her she'd be laughing at this kind of worry in a few years (when her daughter asks to go to the doctor to get the birth control pill!), but when you're in the middle of it, every little thing becomes a massive drama.

The first big decision I had to make as a new mother still fills me with chills. I was a wreck when we decided to have a bris for Josh. Hans is Jewish, and part of the tradition is circumcision on the eighth day of a baby boy's life. I come from an ethnic background where circumcision is rare, and my family was on the phone every day from England telling me how barbaric it was. Meanwhile, friends here told me to get on with it—it was no big deal. They were all wrong.

It was still extremely hot, and the mohel came in the room at the hospital wearing Coke-bottle-bottom glasses, sweat streaming down in front of his eyes, blinding him. As soon as the knife came out, of course, Hans passed out. This time, though, there were no helpful nurses to gently lay him on a bed. I was in no mood for his theatrics, so I left him passed out on the floor. I wasn't going to take my eyes off that knife for a second. Josh let out a scream that I will never forget—I don't care how religious a person is, that baby's shout just pierces a part of you. (In a small reminder of the futility of feeling guilty about things, Josh recently told me he wished we'd kept the flap of foreskin so he could put it in a jar on his shelf—just like his room-mate who keeps his tonsils in a jar by the bed!) After the deed was done, I grabbed my baby, leaving Hans out cold, got in a cab and went home.

When Max came along, we decided to have the bris in our house. Even after that first experience, we knew we couldn't do one and not the other—too many questions in the locker room. We were renovating the house at the time of Max's, and I wiped off a table that had been covered in sawdust. The mohel was finished before we even asked him to begin. Then the strangest thing happened: a dove flew through the window. Everyone was going on about how it was a sign of good fortune. It was probably just a mangy pigeon, but people were very excited, and so we took it as an omen—of what, I wasn't yet sure.

Babies: the Hot New Accessory

There's a cult around pregnancy and parenting these days that is putting more pressure than ever on new mums. "Baby bumps" and babies have become a fashion statement. Partly it's Hollywood's fault, since it's so hot to be a celebrity parent. In the old days, movie stars like Audrey Hepburn, Elizabeth Taylor and Sophia Loren hid their pregnancies, even the fact that they were parents at all, because having a family was looked at as a career killer by the studios. For today's stars, children are the most important accessories. From the day they discover they're pregnant, these women parade around in the chicest outfits, boobs hoisted up like a shelf. Then, days after the birth, they turn up in the gossip mags looking svelte, pushing designer strollers in the park, their babies swaddled in Hermès blankets.

When my kids were small, I cared very little if I wore the same old T-shirt covered with crusty spit-up to the supermarket. I figured I was only going to meet other mums with their similarly uncombed hair and wrinkled clothes who also hadn't slept for weeks. But now it's a different story. The pressure is on for ordinary mothers to have the $2,000 stroller, the poster-boy husband by her side, the charming toddler who smiles up adoringly at her parents in every photo.

All of it sets women up to feel bad about themselves—instead of revelling in the fact that they've created this little life. They start to feel intimidated, as if everyone has it together except for them. But you have to remember that we're seeing those celebrities only at their very best. They've probably spent hours with a team of staff and stylists to make that park outing look so idyllic. I'd like to know where the paparazzi are when that celeb's toddler (inevitably) has a tantrum? Or when the star is looking dishevelled and half stoned from lack of sleep? (It's amazing—those photographers always catch stars when they really are stoned, but never with a red-faced baby crying so hard that he throws up.)

The truth is, whether you're a celeb or just an ordinary mom, you're feeling the same things. You're going to have leaky boobs and emotional ups and downs. You'll feel happy and dreamy one minute and want to dispense with your children (and husband) the next. You're not going to always look gorgeous and glossy. It's just the way it is, and I can tell you for a fact that the little people in your life do not care a toss that you don't prance about like Nicole Richie.

The best way to counter this cult of motherhood is with humour. I learned this watching my own mother and her friends find laughter in the direst situations.

After my father died, my mother needed to find a way to make money. It was impossible for her to go out and get a job with four little kids, the youngest just a baby, so she looked closer to home—literally. We lived in a large five-bedroom home (admittedly, some of the rooms were the size of cupboards), unusual in our area where working-class row houses were the norm, and she decided to take in lodgers from the local electronics factory. They would stay with us from Monday to Friday and return to their own homes in the city on the weekends. She included a hot breakfast, the evening meal and laundry services in the fee.

It must have been back-breaking, but she was young and desperate. One day after school, I was headed out the back door when I heard the strangest screams coming from the bottom of the garden. I raced down to find my mother with a huge pile of laundry, a fistful of clothes pegs and the washing hanging on the line all around her. Our neighbour, Mary, was leaning over the fence as if she was about to be ill. My mother was holding her stomach, her knees buckled. They were laughing so hard that they could barely stand. In Mum's hands was a pair of shiny, skimpy leopard-print men's underpants, a kind unseen outside of London in the early 1970s.

Seeing my mother laughing so hard reassured me that we would be fine. Until we went inside, that is. That night, she was lifting a large shepherd's pie out of the oven when I spotted an empty can of dog food among the dirty pots. We did not have a dog. With the imperious authority of a preteen, I asked her what she thought she was doing. I fell to pieces when she said not to worry, they'd never know with all the carrots and peas mixed in.

"Mum, you cannot feed the lodgers dog food! We'll all go to jail, they'll die!"

It was a very tight week, she explained unapologetically. Twenty minutes later, all three men asked for seconds—which we dutifully served them. The two of us had one of those rare but special mother-daughter moments, and we ended up giggling together like two young girls at her nerve.

Humour and friendship go hand in hand. We all do ridiculously silly things as new mothers, and it takes a good friend to help you find the hilarity in the situation. Because I was new to the city, my only friends when Josh was born were the mothers I met in prenatal class. It was the solitary good thing that came out of those classes, as I found the instruction itself rather pointless. I don't regard being told week after week exactly how much pain we would be in during the birth helped a single bit—it definitely didn't take an ounce of the agony away. And the teacher's suggestion to keep up my sex appeal throughout pregnancy only got me into trouble. In addition to the problem with my tight knickers, Hans broke two toes one evening when we were following her advice.

During the class Miss Simmons (note the Miss—an unmarried prenatal teacher . . .) had passed on some tantalizing tips for keeping our husbands interested in our pregnant bodies. Something to do with a feather duster. That evening, thinking I was being as sensual as a professional pole dancer, I leapt onto the bed, all two hundred pounds of me, feather duster held high. I heard a booming crack and the heavy pine bed frame fell onto Hans's foot. The rest of the night was spent in emergency.

Still, I really valued the other mums I met. We all had our babies at the same time and were able to help each other out. Two weeks after Josh's birth, I drove to the country to see one of these new friends whose little boy Zach had been born on the same day. It was still very hot—stifling, in fact. Josh, dressed in only a diaper, was burbling away as he always did. It was a stark contrast to little Zach who couldn't stop crying. Neither could my friend.

"He's such a strange colour," she complained. "I don't know what to do. I think there's something wrong with him."

I looked at him all wrapped up in mitts and hat, his body swaddled like a burrito. He was as red as a beet.

"You might try taking off the toque," I said, trying to be gentle.

Of course, she was just doing what she thought was right. The nurses had told us to keep them bundled up, and when you're new at being a mum, you regard professional advice as the word of God. It takes a long time to get your confidence as a mother. You forget to trust your instincts because everyone is telling you what to do.

I think we need to let ourselves off the hook and do what works for us. It amazes me how many of today's young mothers seem afraid to let their true feelings out. I know beyond a shadow of a doubt that those strange, sometimes murderous thoughts are completely normal. If you're feeling guilty that you've spanked your four-year-old and are only fit for a ten-year jail sentence, or left little Jamie hanging in the baby bouncer far longer than necessary, your friend probably has a similar tale to tell. Far from judging you, other mothers will likely kick in with their own horror stories of self-doubt and near misses.

Max slid out of the end of his stroller once. I was dreaming away, probably about being single somewhere on a beach with a margarita. I was at least half a block away when a kind gentleman tapped me on the shoulder and handed me my child. Luckily he was in a well-padded snowsuit and was no worse for wear. Still, I ran home racked with shame.

Now I know my guilt was useless. The incident was over. The next time I made sure his stroller straps were on tight. It would be so much better for everyone if we could all just share our stories with a friend over a drink. She probably has a worse one—and if she doesn't, get a new friend.

When the boys were babies, Josh kept refusing his bottle. He'd just push it away, then point at his father. We couldn't figure out what was going on for the longest time and were practically beside ourselves, until we finally realized he was pointing at Hans's Heineken. So I cleaned out a beer bottle, put milk in it and attached a plastic nipple. Josh was happy, and I was happy he was taking the milk again. I got some funny looks when I took my baby out in the pram drinking from a beer bottle (funnier still when Max insisted on copying his brother and was soon propped up beside him having his milk in a Guinness bottle), but whatever kept them content and quiet was all right with me.

Babysitters from Hell

There is one thing that still makes me feel guilty, and that is hiring any type of domestic help. My mother managed to do her own housework, cleaning toilets and doing laundry, and I sometimes think so should I. But the truth is, I hate housework.

As finances improved over the years, my grandest luxury has been to hire a cleaning lady, though even the words *housekeeper, maid* and *domestic* make me squirm with shame in my working-class boots. As for hiring a nanny, I thought I wouldn't even consider it. I would bring up my children by myself—with help from the hubby, of course. But even the best intentions can fall flat, mine a little sooner than expected.

When Josh was six months old, I was already heavily pregnant with Max, and we were undergoing a major renovation to our first home, a rambling brick Victorian that had barely been touched since, well, a Victorian lived in it a hundred years ago. With plaster dust and builders everywhere, I decided to abandon my convictions and hire some babysitting help.

I needed someone I could trust to look after Josh while I ran around picking up tile and other materials. The problem was that the professional nanny agencies were out of our budget range, so I answered an ad stuck in the bread shop window for a "Loving child minder looking to care for someone's precious little one." She sounded as sweet as an English pudding.

I should have known better. At fourteen, I had offered my own babysitting services to every family in my village. The plan was to save enough money so I could go on a summer holiday with my best friend and her parents to Torquay on the south coast of England. It wasn't exactly the Caribbean, but that sleepy seaside town packed with retirees, their legs wrapped in woolly blankets, became a heaving mass of discos, chippies and pubs in the summer months. We figured it was the ideal place to meet hordes of lads.

That year, I spent countless evenings ignoring whingeing children while I chatted up every boy on the block on the family's phone and swigged sherry from their stash. I found the whole babysitting thing unbelievably dull. Still, I managed to raise the money to go to Torquay plus £100 of pocket money.

My best friend, Rosy, and I were thrilled. When we arrived, the two of us were given the worst room in the seafront bed and breakfast. It was not only tiny but right next to the kitchen in the basement of an Edwardian monstrosity. Not that we cared. In fact, it was ideal for sneaking in and out at all hours without her parents clueing in.

Going out on the prowl required a flurry of outfit changes, masses of makeup trials and primping of hair. Unfortunately, we only had one electrical socket in our little room. One night, in order to speed up the process, I grabbed my hair dryer and went out to the hallway. I blithely unplugged whatever was in the socket and was soon looking like something out of the pages of a teen magazine.

The night out was a success, we danced for hours and even scored a few kisses behind the bus stop with some local lads, but breakfast in the stodgy dining room the next morning was a fright. The beloved cooked English breakfast had been replaced with cereal. (Wars have started over less in the British Isles.) Someone, it turned out, had unplugged the hotel freezer the previous evening and everything had been lost. It didn't take much detective work to find the culprit, and every penny of that hard-won babysitting money was gone.

But even remembering my own babysitting years, when Sharmaine the "loving child minder" from Liverpool stumbled up our steps for the first time, I had to contain my shock. She was a little on the chubby side, with a very short skirt leaving nothing to the imagination. Her wool tights were fashionably ripped, punk-style, and she dragged in a puddle of mud on the bottom of her knee-high laced-up Doc Martens. Still, the price was right—she'd come to North America to travel and had run out of money so would work for just room and board—and I was simply grateful to have a reprieve. By the time Hans got home that night, I had got over the tattoos and green gem in her front tooth (I actually thought it was a piece of spinach).

I didn't even mind that she took the only bedroom

that was finished from the renovation. After all, I had to keep her happy—she was going to be watching my baby. And I was okay with her taking a break after spending the morning talking to the other British nannies in the park— she had to catch up on her soaps. And, of course, as she was allergic to laundry soap and dishwashing liquid, poor dear, I could hardly insist that she help out on that front. Even spending her evenings and most of the night out meeting fellow Brits in every club in the city was okay with me—a girl needs to let loose sometimes.

But as the weeks went by, I started to wonder if Sharmaine might think of picking up a few things at the grocery store when she was out and about with Josh in his stroller. If perhaps she might cut into her soap time to get him up from his nap. My complaints started to build, but Hans didn't want to hear about it. He was out the door as fast as possible each morning, headed for the sanctuary of his office.

It all came to an ugly end one morning when Sharmaine was hungover from her clubbing. Like an idiot, I lumbered up the stairs, pregnant, Josh in one arm, a tray of tea, toast and marmalade—her favourite—in the other. She was sitting up in bed, moaning about her aching head, as I presented Her Highness with breakfast.

Just then, Hans came home unexpectedly. He'd popped in to check on the contractor and witnessed the crazy scene, his pregnant wife prostrate at the altar of the Liverpudlian punk. In a flurry of obscenities and ripped tights, Sharmaine was out the door.

When Max was born, the daily routine became more difficult for all of us. He was a tougher baby because he cried more, and I was tired and stressed from chasing a toddler around and trying to keep them both happy. It was only really then that my mother's death hit me. Not having her there to talk to was painful.

Of course, I was also exhausted. Pregnant women are always saying, "I'm so tired," but once you've had a couple of children you just have to laugh. The truth is that it never goes away. You give up sleep when you have kids. Now that my children are grown, I'm in bed at 11 p.m., but *they're* just getting ready to go out. I'll spend two hours listening to their hair dryers and fights over styling gel, then finally hear the door slam, only to be woken from the deepest dream at 4 a.m. when they come in with their friends, whispering so loudly that the whole street can hear them. That sleep deprivation never goes away.

And it begins with the newborn. Every time you boast to your friends that your darling child is sleeping six hours straight, wham! the routine is turned on its ass, and they're sleeping all day and wanting to play all night. The maddening part is that everyone—including the milkman—has a theory on how to get them to have a solid night's sleep. I know couples who have nearly split up or killed each other over the "Let them cry it out" routine. You're supposed to let them go for two minutes before you comfort them, then five, then ten, until eventually they are supposed to comfort themselves. But it's more a game of who can outwit and outlast the other. Usually the parents give in first. I once found Hans curled up inside the crib fast asleep beside his son—now that was a fun habit to break!

Josh was a great sleeper, just not in his own bed. When he was in a crib we would lie in our room down the hall listening to him build up his bounce with the precision of an Olympic trampolinist. He'd jump and jump, then we'd hear the inevitable thump as he hit the floor. Then he'd take off at a crawl toward our room. Most of the time we were just too bloody exhausted to fight it. Even now, a six-foot-tall rugby player, he thinks nothing of snuggling in for a cuddle with Hans and me.

We eventually bought the highest four-poster bed we could find. Josh devised every strategy to pull himself up like a thief scaling a wall. When he couldn't make it, he'd curl up like a dog under the bed. It got so bad that we put a lock on our door, but he just ended up sleeping on the floor in the hallway. Next, we moved the lock to the outside of his door. (I'm sure children's services would have something to say about that—probably haul me away in a second.) We finally gave up when he started to tunnel his way out through the wall he shared with the bathroom. We had been defeated.

Birth-Order Roulette

It never ceases to amaze me that children who come from the same parents can end up so incredibly different in so many ways. When you're pregnant, you look at yourself and your partner and with fingers crossed pray that the child will take the best genes from each of you. I always thought that if I had a little girl I would have called her Lily. It's such a pretty name, but she could very well have ended up built like Hans with a wide chest and narrow hips, or a hairy back. How your kids turn out physically is a crapshoot.

When our boys were small, they were so close in age that they seemed almost like twins. We'd often put them in the same bed and they'd wake up sucking each other's thumb, but it always amazed me how completely different they were from one another.

From the time he could propel himself, Josh was a really active child, always moving, quite clumsy. He didn't just crawl, he bounced. He's still that way. He plays rugby and American football and has broken more limbs than most people have eaten hot dinners. Since he was young, he's had this fascination with the Second World War (I wonder now if his late-night strategizing about how to get out of his own bedroom was the spark that lit his passion!). At fourteen, he and Hans took a two-week trip to visit all the concentration camps in Germany. He's now doing war studies at King's College at London University.

Max, on the other hand, is incredibly independent. From the beginning he adored his own bed, his own space. That has never wavered. Today, he's specializing in media and film at university. He's athletic, too, and artistic, but very different from his brother. I look at them and see so clearly how much of who a child becomes depends on birth order.

I definitely see it with my own siblings. I'm the typical, bossy did-everything-first eldest child. My second sister, Joanna, was the follower, trying to make her own mark in the world (at her wedding, she turned around at the altar and whispered, "See! I did it before you!"). As an adult, she came into her own and always can be counted on to see the bright side of things. Emma was the easygoing third child, and to this day looks for the less complicated route through life. And of course, my brother, the longed-for male, was godlike. We smothered him when we were girls. He was our living, breathing Barbie doll. He might have turned out to have a fetish for women's clothing and high-heeled shoes, but thankfully he's a really cool guy who only dresses up on the weekend (just kidding). My mother shipped him off to an all-boys boarding school to give him a break from all the females surrounding him.

I look at my own boys now—so different from each other but both strong, healthy young men beginning their own lives—and I can hardly believe they were little babies, that all I remember (and so much that I've forgotten) really happened. There's one event, though, that I have no trouble recalling. It was the most frightening, life-altering experience that has ever happened to me. The boys were still really young, just two and three. It permanently changed the way I viewed the smaller annoyances that life inevitably threw at me. I would forever see the larger picture.

Why are kids so mean? At first, you think it's cute. Guests chuckle when you ask your scrumptious little lad clutching a bag of sweets in his tight little fist if you can have one of his Smarties. He painfully removes one—never two—and hands it over. Everyone claps, he loves the acclaim, but it's clear that deep down he's not happy. Sixteen years later, the same boy is glaring at you when you suggest he should use some of the money he earned working over the summer as pocket money on vacation. "But that's my money, I earned it," he says—as if *you* didn't *earn* yours. Take a few Halloween candies out of the pillowcase they've stuffed them in—the ones they've counted to the last jelly bean—or pinch a fry off their plate, or ask for even the smallest lick of their ice cream and you are guaranteed an "Oh, Mum, can't you get your own?" If any child psychologist has the answer to ending this perennial mean reflex, I would love to hear it. In the meantime I'll have to just keep trying—*"Come on, give us a bit of your takeout while I write out more college cheques."*

3

Why is the sky blue, and other annoying questions

It is utterly baffling to me how we adults manage to do the many things we do in our daily lives—organize mortgages, hold dinner parties for twenty, find our way around mega-markets, get to and from our offices—and think nothing of it. But throw a two-year-old into the mix and the whole carefully constructed house of cards comes crashing down. They are like little tyrants, always testing exactly how much power they have, how far they can go, how much they can push you before you snap. For the first time in their young lives, they're stepping away from their parents, asserting themselves, and like drunks who don't know when to back down from a fight, they will push and push and push.

I was reminded of this one evening recently when I found my friend Helen on my doorstep clutching the usual bottle of wine. She didn't need to say a word. "You'd better come in," I said in a voice designed to soothe her scowl.

Helen lives next door. She is a physician and professor of medicine at a major teaching hospital. I admire her tremendously, though we're like oil and water—utterly different. She's really clever and I'm not. I'm English, she's Irish. We're close in age, but Helen's two kids are still young, whereas I'm in the home stretch. We live in totally dissimilar worlds, but we're there for each other, especially when one of us wants to throw in the towel.

Her youngest is an angelic, doll-faced toddler named Lauren. Each morning, Helen drops her off at the daycare in the hospital where she works. It sounds like an idyllic setup for a busy working mum, but no morning goes by without some form of confrontation.

"The debates are worse than in my office," Helen says over gulps of chardonnay. Most of it is about clothing. Her daughter is a fashionista, the sort who's worn more outfits at two years old than most supermodels do in a lifetime.

"There are surgeons ready to start their day, patients waiting in operating theatres across the hospital, but everything has to stop dead because I made a stupid mistake," Helen explains, her Irish accent growing thicker as she sips her wine. "This morning, when we walked into the daycare, I just happened to mention to Lauren that she was wearing mismatched shoes. Well, I'm surprised the cardiac machines didn't explode with the decibel of her screams. She threw off every item of clothing she was wearing, put it all back on in a new configuration, topping it off with her mismatched shoes on the wrong feet—just to make a point.

"She looked like a miniature bag lady. I told her to have a lovely day, and ran crying for the sanctuary of the operating theatre."

Dealing with a toddler is very much like facing an opposing army. It came too late for my own purposes, but thanks to my eldest child and his longtime interest in the Second World War, I now know a thing or two about strategy, and I'm here to say that the experts who tell parents they should get down to their toddler's level to "discuss matters" are just plain wrong. If any soldier had to confront the enemy on her knees, she would be at a major disadvantage—especially if that enemy has a scream that can crack windows and a kick worthy of a black belt.

Bravery is your most important weapon. In the morning, when they wake up and run for headquarters—your marital bed—don't be fooled. Those smiling early-morning faces, cuddles and kisses are mere camouflage: the true foe will expose himself well before breakfast.

Each day brings a new skirmish. You may win, but you will probably lose. Even size isn't in your favour since your two-foot opponent can twist and turn with the speed and agility of a ninja, will break every rule on biting and definitely hits below the belt. They have also mastered the element of surprise.

I learned this when I nearly died at the tender age of thirty-one. It was a beautiful sunny winter's day. The whole family was outside digging and clearing snow. I sat on the front steps watching Hans shovel the path while Max pushed the snow right back down it—a scene straight out of a Norman Rockwell painting.

Josh was nowhere to be seen until, without warning, he walked up behind me and hit me over the head with a hammer. "Look, Mummy's a boiled eggy!" he announced, laughing with glee. "What the fu . . . ?" Hans screamed as I slid, semi-conscious, down our front steps.

Max leapt on my inert body. "Me play too!"

Fortunately, I came to within seconds, and have no permanent damage (well, not much). We put it down to overexuberance, an accident, but sometimes I am not so sure. That sweet little face peering down at me—"Mummy has a big bump!"—looked suspiciously knowing.

The truth is, I have always expected to wake up one morning and discover that my children are actually crazed aliens from a planet of very short people. To deal with such a foe, coming up with effective strategies just makes good sense. War measures. And this means that in addition to extreme bravery, you will need to have a stash of projectile-type weapons. When you're on the phone, for instance, and they are interrupting you—as they will inevitably do—I've found throwing anything near to hand works quite well. You pitch a tennis ball or the phone book at them, followed by a withering stare, the Look, which says, One more word and your whole life is cancelled.

Probably my favourite weapon of all, though, is the word *no*. I think of it like a yoga mantra. They'll be asking, "Mum, can I have . . . ?" "Mum, can I go . . ." "I need money . . ." and I'll just block it all out, keep flicking through a magazine. It's actually very relaxing once you get the hang of it. Just keep repeating "No, no, no . . ." in a normal voice. They'll soon grow bored (and move on to the next demand).

Aprons On, Boys—It's Craft Time!

When my lads were toddlers, I started getting desperate to do something other than pick up toys and change full diapers. As it is for any mum, going back to work was a hard and emotional decision. You're desperate for human contact that doesn't involve discussing the merits of breastfeeding versus formula, but you don't want to miss a minute of that precious time with your children. It can be a dreadful tug-of-war playing out in your mind—should I or shouldn't I go back to work?

The key is to absolutely trust your instinct about what feels right. You may well be surprised at yourself. While you were pregnant you might have dreamed about spending the rest of your days contentedly counting out Cheerios, but after only a few months you feel completely stir-crazy. And I know many high-powered career women who thought they'd go back to work straightaway, only to find themselves wanting to dedicate their lives to bake sales and the playground. Of course, even being able to make such a decision is for the lucky ones—so many mothers don't have a choice at all; they simply have to return to their jobs to make ends meet.

In the end, for me, getting back to work was something of an accident. It all began in my kitchen among the piles of dirty dishes and building blocks.

Decorative painting—an ancient art form that involves reproducing the look of grand stone and exquisite wood using only paint—had exploded in the British design world in the late 1980s. Barely a home remained untouched, as everyone tried his or her hand at making baseboards look like marble or a wall colour resemble the patina on a Tuscan villa. The fever, however, had yet to reach North America.

I began by experimenting with paint in the old Victorian house we'd just restored. I practised on the kitchen table on large white boards while the children played around my feet. It was a real matter of trial and error. Over and over again, I would try to achieve the right mixture of linseed oil, oil paint and turpentine. Today, there are water-based paints that do the same job, but at the time our house smelled like a car spray shop.

I loved everything about it. I was in my own little world experimenting away. I began to research what few European books there were and found the subject fascinated me. I discovered that paint had always been the poor man's design tool. On the east coast of the United States in the 1800s, travelling artisans would offer their services emulating the fine woods of Europe. They'd paint homemade trunks made of cheap pine so they resembled walnut, mahogany and chestnut. They'd use vinegar and beer to produce glazes that could recreate the lustre and pattern of tortoiseshell and marble.

It made sense that this time around, as well, decorative painting had taken off with average people: it doesn't require the talents of a fine artist, but it's also not the tedious chore of painting with a roller. The more I experimented, the more I enjoyed it—I think there's an immense energy and confidence that you get when you teach yourself something. It felt to me as if the sky was the limit (and, in fact, I became an expert at painting every type of fluffy cloud and sky!).

Once I'd mastered a technique on those white boards, I would give it a try it on my walls. Our home literally became my canvas. Each effect was not necessarily a hit first time around. One of the worst rows Hans and I ever had was at four in the morning during those early days. I was determined to make our dining room walls look exactly like rich leather panels in the deepest red. I had started painting the previous morning and was still trying to get it right in the middle of the night.

"Oh for God's sake, give it up!" Hans shouted, standing in his boxers with the moon shining through the windows. "Can't you just buy some wallpaper like a normal person?"

"I'm nearly there," I tried to explain, the floor around me littered with filthy rags and dozens of ice-cream cartons (I had become a familiar fixture in the neighbourhood digging around in everyone's recycling bins looking for these cartons because they were the perfect size for mixing colours).

"You'll never be able to handle the kids tomorrow," he needled, while I imagined myself pouring paint thinner in his morning coffee.

I never did master those leather panels, but I kept at my hobby, turning into something of a woman possessed, working away at perfecting my technique while the kids happily mucked around with me all day. The three of us actually looked forward to Hans—the doubting Thomas—leaving in the morning. The minute he fled down the driveway, it was sleeves rolled up and "Aprons on, boys—it's craft time!"

When our friends saw the kind of effeccts I could create with paint, word began to get out, and I started receiving calls asking me to use my newfound skills in other people's homes. It was a good thing because we needed the money. Hans had broken up with his business partner and finances were shaky.

But as the work grew, I found I could no longer take the boys with me to play on someone's floor while I was up the ladder. Some of my clients were extremely wealthy, and I had to become professional overnight. I needed help.

I had steered away from nannies since the fiasco with Sharmaine, the punk rocker, but I was desperate. In walked Elvy, a beautiful young woman from the Philippines. She was ideal. The boys adored her. She cooked and attacked the mountains of laundry with a smile on her face. My only problem with the arrangement was that the most important person in her world was "Mr. Hans." Every afternoon at four, the children happily planted in front of the television, all jobs stopped and her makeover began. Off came the rubber gloves and apron, on went the rollers, the smoky eyeshadow and good clothes. The procedure would take until about five-thirty, when the master returned. She served Hans his meal while I fed the kids. I thought it was pretty odd—but I wasn't going to grumble too much because Elvy's presence gave me some freedom.

Starting to work in other people's homes was a real eye-opener for me. Some clients were wonderful and became friends as they sat on the bottom of my ladder chatting and laughing, then making me lunch. Others, it seemed, looked down on me. They called me the Painter, and rarely even asked if I wanted a glass of water. Once, during this painting period, I was waiting to pick up my kids in the playground at their well-established boys' school, one of the other mothers—who'd been a client at one time—stared at me, rather disturbed, and asked what I was doing there. "Are you painting the school?" she said. When I told her that my children were students there, she looked as if she'd stepped in something nasty.

There were lots of other people who were amazing and supportive. Occasionally I had to bring the kids with me because the sitter was sick, and they'd just plop down and watch me paint. They became superb little helpers. One lovely client played with them after school each day while I painted her crown mouldings to look like tortoiseshell.

Fifteen years later, after a rather acrimonious divorce, she was left with very little and approached me for a job. Today, she's one of my best researchers at our TV production studio. (The more I see in my life, the more the idea *What goes around comes around* makes sense to me.)

Even though the kids had a mummy who had the lingering odour of a paint factory about her, things were going well at home, and my business was thriving. Organization was the key. I planned to be at a job site for a maximum of six hours a day. That meant being sure that every rag, brush and ladder I would need was in my truck. There was no time for mistakes. If I forgot a crucial tool, I either had to spend money to replace it or return home—both a complete waste of time.

As a young working mum, I found time precious—not something I was willing to squander. My trick was that every morning I would lie in bed and walk through the day's job in my head. As I imagined each step and tool and product needed, I would mentally tick it off my list. It worked like a dream and I rarely forgot anything.

I was careful, meticulous even, and made sure my materials were safely out of reach of my toddlers, but one hot summer's day I slipped up. I often mixed my own colours. I would take a small squirt from a tube of pure artist's oil, then break it down with a little thinner and pour the mixture into a tin of glaze. The pigment was so powerful that one little blob could colour an entire room.

That day I was up a ladder out on our deck painting the

top part of an armoire. One-year-old Max was inside with Hans, while Josh played happily—stark naked—on the deck below me. I turned my back for a second, and when I looked down I saw he had managed to open the tube of cobalt blue—one of the most toxic colours there is. He looked like something from the Blue Man Group. It was in his hair, under his fingernails and rubbed all over his precious little body.

The only sure method to remove oil paint is with paint thinner, but I couldn't use that on Josh's fresh young skin, so I doused him in olive oil. For weeks, I rubbed him with oil until he was slick (he still has beautiful, succulent skin). But the intense colour faded slowly. He had this strange blue tint for weeks.

Accidents like that you've got to laugh about. But sometimes something happens in a family that is far from comical.

When Things Go Wrong

March 12, 1991. I woke up to the sound of retching. Up to that point, my kids had rarely been sick. (I figured they must have their mother's constitution—I have never had a cold in my life and have entertained several offers to leave my body to science.) But that day, I went into their shared room to find little Max, just two years old, projectile vomiting with such force it that was hitting the far wall. The previous day I had stencilled their bedroom walls with knights and dragons, and my first thought on seeing the

gooey mess was that all my work was ruined. Quickly coming to my senses, I swept Max up in my arms and said to
Josh, "Help Mummy and grab a towel. You can clean off
the dragons."

I was alarmed by Max's throwing up, of course, but not
hugely worried at that point. He actually looked incredibly
healthy with bright rosy cheeks. He seemed to be glowing.

I was supposed to be painting a mural on a wealthy
client's dining room ceiling that morning, so I rang her to
say one of my kids was sick and would she mind if I came
the following day. Well, the woman whined like a spoiled
toddler about how her dinner party was going to be ruined
if it wasn't finished. I listened to her as she shouted down
the phone, all the while looking at this sweet little boy
slumped on our bed. "I'm sorry I dirtied the George and the
Dragons," he mumbled. The lump in my throat felt like a
grapefruit. Gut instinct took over. "I'll be there tomorrow,"
I said and hung up. (I never did finish that job.)

By that point Max was lying down and seemed to be
sleeping deeply. I still wasn't overly concerned—what person
wouldn't be exhausted after throwing up like that? I called
out to my little helper, Josh, who was happily scrubbing
down the bedroom wall with a pair of his father's underpants.

"Could you grab me the thermometer?" I asked. (The
kids loved taking each other's temperature in those days.
If you'd asked me then about their future careers I would
have sworn they would have both been in medical school
by now.) He dutifully brought it, and I placed it in Max's

mouth. His temperature was 105°F—off the charts high. I realized then that try as I might, I couldn't wake him.

Attempting to contain my rising panic and not willing to leave Max's side, I said, "Okay, Josh, you know how I showed you how to dial 911? Off you go and dial it, then bring me the phone." It was the longest five minutes of my life while he tottered off and then back in. "Is the nine the tadpole one? Like a head with a tail?" he asked, holding up the phone.

For some reason, in that moment, all my calmness melted away. I called Hans. He was in a meeting with the bank and he raced home to get us. We drove to our doctor, who took one look at him and sent us straight to the Children's Hospital. We were there in minutes. Emergency was swarming with white-coated doctors and nurses. I thought there must have been a huge car accident or some other tragedy that they were waiting to deal with. I was already complaining to myself that we would be waiting for hours, when Max was abruptly whisked out of my arms and into an isolated room, the white coats following behind.

Within a few minutes, someone ran past carrying what looked like a pneumatic drill. Great, I thought, still grumpy about the busy hospital and the wait we'd no doubt have to endure, they're renovating. Could our timing be any worse? The man—who it turned out was a male nurse—must have known we were wondering what he was doing because he paused and said that we must stay calm, but they were going to drill a hole in Max's head to release the pressure that had built up. There had been a serious outbreak of bacterial meningitis in the area, and they thought he might be one of the victims. All the people rushing around, it turned out, were there for us.

My life changed irreversibly in that moment. We were to spend the next four months in the Children's Hospital, with a very uncertain future. I don't think you can go through something like that and not come out changed. Every time an upsetting event happens in our family life, I just think back to those terrifying days and months, and all the ordinary daily drama comes into perspective. If we could survive that, we could survive anything.

Max was in a coma. I remember waiting at the closed doors of the operating room thinking how everything had changed so quickly. Just the day before he'd been running around happily with his big brother, and now he was in critical care fighting for his life. We had been catapulted into another world. I don't think Hans or I ate for a week. If someone had come and told us we had won millions in the lottery or that they were going to hack off our legs, I'm pretty sure we wouldn't have known the difference. The clock had stopped.

Max had four brain operations over four months as a result of the meningitis. Without a doubt those doctors saved his life.

We stayed with him the whole time he was in the hospital. We fell into a routine of having me doing the day shift while Hans tried to work; at night, Hans would sleep on the floor next to Max's hospital bed while I rushed home to be with Josh.

Every mother has a stack of things she feels guilty about. The tears in the knees of your kids' jeans, not volunteering enough at the school, working too hard, et cetera, et cetera. Most of it is a complete waste of energy. We spend way too much time obsessing, feeling bad about something we've done or failed to do, but even after seventeen years my feelings of guilt about this incident can stop me cold.

I hadn't taken vaccines very seriously with my children. I'd given them all the compulsory ones, but I often lost that little book the pediatrician gives you to keep track. You see, I didn't have vaccinations at all when I was a child. My mother didn't believe in them. Her reasoning was justified at the time: when I was young the whooping cough vaccine caused some highly publicized cases of brain damage, even death, and the U.K. was still reeling from the thalidomide disaster, in which mothers given a drug for morning sickness gave birth to children with serious deformities. People were suspicious of medicines in general and many children were not inoculated at all. We actually went to chicken pox and German measles parties in our village so all the children would get the infections together and be immune for life.

When my kids were small, the meningitis vaccine was a relatively new offering, and I had never got around to getting it for my boys. I'm not a vaccination fanatic one way or the other now—there's a lot of research out there and more, I'm sure, to be done—but in the case of Max and meningitis, I was wrong to be so lax, and I've never stopped feeling the pain and terror of that situation. We were lucky that he survived with nothing more than a nasty scar hidden in his unruly mop of hair—several children died in the area that spring.

Welcome to My World

The great thing about having a family and being busy with the daily routine of home and work is that even when life seems horrible, it just keeps rolling on. If life is a bit pissy today, just wait. It's like the weather in England: if you don't like it, wait a minute and it's sure to change.

It wasn't long after Max came home from the hospital and our lives resumed some form of normalcy that my painting business really began to take off. Word had spread, and suddenly I was inundated with painting commissions at synagogues and department stores, theatres, auditoriums and big fancy mansions. I was becoming the Michelangelo of our neighbourhood. I even had to find other artists to work for me because the jobs were too big to do alone. But I found it was like keeping the patrons happy at a favourite restaurant: diners want to see the chef, and my clients needed to see me there on-site, brush in hand. I found being in people's homes was a little like being a hairdresser—I heard their secrets and saw how other families behaved.

I loved it, but it was also hard physical work. I never seemed to get out of my overalls. There was Elvy, my pristine, perfectly coiffed housekeeper, calmly helping with the children, while I went around looking like Bob the Builder—not exactly a Yummy Mummy!

I was drained at the end of a day after painting the sky on someone else's child's ceiling or spending hours balancing on a scaffold fixing gold leaf in a church. Now it was me, not just Hans, who came home exhausted, needing time to clean up before tackling the kids, hoping for a second to at least clean the paint out from underneath my fingernails. As work really started to take off for me, Hans was very supportive. Our relationship was good before Max's illness, but that experience of going hand in hand to hell and back cemented us together forever. We knew even more clearly that we could work well as a team and that we'd do it until we're in our graves.

Each night before bed, even when I was completely spent, the kids and I would read a story together. It always seemed to be the same old book about bunnies or turtles again and again. Just to break up the monotony, I'd improvise. "The bunny went up the ladder with his sponge and started painting the ceiling," I'd pretend to read. The boys would holler, "That's not right!" But they loved it.

Kids want to be included in their parents' world. But, also, telling them about your work or your day helps them understand that you have a life away from them. It's easy when you're little to think that the world revolves around you and that everyone is there solely to meet your needs. I actually remember feeling that way myself, and being brought back to reality by my mother screaming (God knows what I'd done that time!) that it was not all about me–that other people mattered, as well. I was genuinely surprised.

Even more, telling them about the stuff you do outside your home–even the frustrations and difficulties–they'll begin to understand that when you're tired or grumpy at the end of the day, it's probably not about *them* at all. Kids blame themselves for every situation and mood in their home. If you're snapping at everyone while you prepare dinner, they will likely assume it's something they've done.

You can include them in talk about your work life no matter what age your kids are. They'll love to laugh at how someone dropped his soup on the floor at lunchtime or how Mr. Jones came in from the pouring rain and his big hairy moustache was dripping on Mrs. Smith's head. And if you're a stay-at-home mum, tales of what happened in the park or an argument at the dry cleaners can be equally interesting to little ears.

I have always been a huge advocate of the evening meal, sitting down together around the table. Even if the fare is not a home-cooked wonder, it's one moment in the day when everyone can breathe together as a family and be part of one another's world. It's a chance to get away from all the chaos of rushing in from work, banging pots and pans, racing off to after-school programs and all the other busyness that fills our lives.

Nursery School Failure

When Josh and then Max turned four, I enrolled them in preschool. It was the sort of place that went from nine to eleven every morning, and parents who worked could pay extra to keep kids there for a few more hours. The other mothers would drop their children off and head to aerobics class or yoga, then back to the preschool, while I'd be up a ladder in my paint-splotched overalls until I raced to get them at the last possible minute. For new parents, the place seemed as important to their future as their senior year in high school.

At the end of each term, the little school gave out report cards. When the first one arrived, Hans and I opened the envelope with the nervous tension of an Oscar nominee. We scanned the page and sighed with relief: Josh had done well. We could breathe easily with the smug superiority of parents of an honour student. He played well with others and he shone at building blocks. But then we noticed something scrawled at the bottom of the page: it was a big bloody F. Our son, our firstborn, had failed sandboxing.

I didn't know what to do. We went through the possible reasons, the implications. Josh's future ran through my mind like a film in fast forward: I was weeping in front of the principal, begging him to let Josh pass high school, I was bailing him out of jail, I was bringing him blankets where he lived on the street. Even Hans was rattled. "Maybe we should think about tutoring?"

We were truly horrified. I considered bringing it up with the other mothers I'd befriended but couldn't bear to admit our private shame.

It was absurd, even pathetic, and we soon moved on, but all new parents have those moments. You think that whatever has happened—whether it's an F in sandboxing or your child biting another one or yelling filthy words in public (where did he hear that, anyway?)—will dog him forever. But as anyone with older children will delight in telling you, not only will you forget, but you'll laugh at yourself for taking it so seriously. And anyway, you don't know the half of it. The mum with the new baby pooh-poohs the pregnant woman's worries; the busy working woman with a houseful of teenagers thinks the one with toddlers has it easy.

It never seems that way at the time, of course—like when you've got three- and four-year-olds and you can't walk a step without being asked head-splitting, unanswerable questions. Max fell asleep as soon as he was strapped in his carseat, arriving bright and cheery wherever we were going, but Josh would chirp away the entire trip: "Is Daddy having a baby, Mummy? Why is his tummy so fat?" "Why is the sky blue?" "Why can't I fly?" My head would be spinning.

At home, with both of them awake, the questions would come in stereo. The worst was when "How was I born?" became "Were we really found behind a bush?" and "Jake says that babies come out of your nose." For several weeks, they became hooked on adoption. "Mum, I think we were adopted," "Mummy? Was I adopted? I don't look like anyone else in the family" and then, of course, "It's not fair if he was adopted and I wasn't."

Finally, one bath time as their crazy-making rant continued, I threw my bubble-covered arms in the air and said, "Look, do you really think if I was going to adopt children I would have picked you lot? There are a couple of pretty little rich girls up the road I could have chosen." I don't think they ever asked again.

Vacations Are for Fools

So you think you have a routine. Things are running pretty smoothly. Kids off to preschool, you've found a fairly clean shirt at the bottom of the laundry basket, chicken is ready for the oven when you get home. You've set it all up, and no, it's not easy, but you're managing. Try to transport that familiar routine to your holiday, and the dirty diapers hit the fan. Chaos in the castle has nothing on panic on the plane, the train or the dreaded overstuffed automobile driven by desperate Dad.

When my children were small, I longed to spend time with my siblings in England, so back and forth we went like a pack of mules. I was usually on my own since Hans had to work (or that's the excuse he gave). There are no doubt passengers out there somewhere in the world who still bear the scars of having the bad luck to be on the same plane as my two boys and me. Although they were generally superb sleepers at home (when Josh could get out of his own bed, anyway), they never, ever slept on a long flight. They were simply too excited.

Who wouldn't be when you can play hide-and-seek and Mum never finds you?

And all those pretty ladies in blue uniforms and funny hats who crawl along the aisles looking under the seats—it's so much fun! There are people to play with, row upon row of interested adults to talk to. And there's that bassinette that hangs on the wall in the front row—if you jump on it hard enough, it will pull out of the wall and crush your brother playing underneath! But the best of all is the trolley that whizzes up and down the aisle if you push it really hard.

Then there's Mum. She always carries loads of candies—doling them out especially when she's crying, which she seems to do constantly on the plane. And she brings masses of toys and games. The only problem is she gets so cross sometimes that she says she'll need Botox from all the scowling. One time she was so furious when the lady in the blue told her to go to the front of the plane and be quiet and breathe. *She* got sent to the naughty corner for once. You try to make her feel better by cutting out her nice picture from the little blue book that the man at customs stamps, but even that doesn't stop her screaming. What a fuss she makes!

One time, when the boys were toddlers, my stepfather and his wife, Elizabeth, lent us their holiday apartment in the Costa Brava in Spain. The one condition was that under no circumstances would they be required to be there at the same time. We knew it was going to be a long journey—an eight-hour flight to Madrid, then another plane to Barcelona, followed by a three-hour car trip—and I was in a state of panic. Even though Hans was going with us this time, the thought of dealing with the kids for twenty-four hours of travel time was causing me facial tics. As I packed up the last bag containing the entire contents of our home, Max reached in and scooped up his little round green goggles. This was the Ninja Turtle era, and every boy under six was either Leonardo, Michelangelo or whatshisface. Max is a very stubborn kid, and I was too exasperated and exhausted to argue. He put them on in our house and didn't take them off for the entire vacation. He looked like a little green frog.

In my terror about our long journey, I had asked a friend for advice about travelling so far with little kids. She suggested a teaspoon of Gravol to help them sleep on the plane. Brilliant idea, I thought. As we were leaving the house, I gave each of the boys a dose from the bottle. Then another. I thought I was unbelievably clever. They didn't wake up until we pulled into my stepfather's driveway a full day and night later.

My head burst with pride when, for the first time, other passengers on the plane came up to me with comments like, "Your children are marvellous! Such good travellers!" I smiled, though I thought, *I just hope they're not dead.*

The biggest hitch was our carry-on luggage. I am always worried about checking important items in case they get lost, so I'd brought a gigantic bag of diapers with us. "You never know," I explained as we ran through several airports lugging them along. "They may not sell diapers or Band-Aids in Spain."

The kids, meanwhile, were comatose in one of those double strollers where they sit side by side, and I had all our belongings hanging from the handles: our enormous video camera, bags with enough clothes for forty different climate changes and diapers sufficient to supply a small country. The boys were so heavily sedated that they were like dead weight. If we tried to lift one of them out, the whole stroller would flip over because of all the stuff loaded on the handles.

Twenty-four hours later, we arrived all in one piece, but as we unlocked the front door the children woke up. They stayed awake for the rest of the week. Let me tell you, there is nothing like playing on a Spanish beach at three in the morning.

I don't suggest people drug their kids for the purely selfish desire for a peaceful flight (though I did get to drink champagne and read a book). But you do need to adjust travel plans to the age of your children. Being overly ambitious when they're little will always come back to bite you.

Even the places that are geared to kids can be difficult. There is nothing like the wonder of Disney World, but even in the Magic Kingdom there are agitated mothers hissing at their children, "What's wrong with you? You have to be happy! Every *other* child is having a good time.

SMILE or we're going home right now!" That constant overload of fun and food is guaranteed to cause plenty of whining.

Simple is nearly always the best way to go. One of my favourite vacations when I was a child was the time my parents borrowed a relative's converted cow barn smack in the middle of a field. There wasn't even a road leading up to it, so we had to lug our bags through high grass just to get there. It was pure, easy fun—especially since the cows ignored the fact that the barn had been renovated as a house and tried to wander in at every opportunity. Of course, our fun was my mother's work. She had to pump water for the kitchen, and the place smelled like manure. Everyday chores became monumental. At the time, we just thought she was a party-pooper, going around the entire holiday mumbling "Never again" under her breath.

It's the same for some of my friends who pack up their household each weekend to spend time roughing it at the cottage. They fight the traffic with screaming children in the back seat, then *still* have to cook and clean.

When you're a kid, all you really need on vacation is other kids, maybe some sand, mud and water. We once stayed at a luxurious hotel in Jamaica over spring break. It was quite posh, and it had every possible amenity for the fun-loving family. Heinrich the German "games organizer" had the important job of making sure that everyone "vos having a vunderful time." He really was a stunning specimen strutting that beach in his lemon yellow Speedo.

On the first day, our boys spotted a huge, leggy crab the size of a baseball glove, and chased it into a drain beneath a path that led to the beach. They spent the rest of the week poking sticks at the poor creature hiding inside, an ever-growing entourage of other vacationing children tagging along behind. That crab kept them occupied from morning until night—to the frustration of poor Heinrich, who tried so desperately to persuade the kids to have some *real* fun. He raced by on the inflated banana boat, waved from parachutes and somersaulted up and down the beach. "Come on, kinders, ve MUST have fun!" he shrieked. But even Heinrich couldn't compete with a crab and a stick.

The other day, I watched my neighbour, who's the vice-president of a major company, leaning over a pot of peas with the intensity she might bring to discussions of a company merger. Her suit still on from work, she stood at the stove, the three dinner plates she'd just grabbed from her children in hand, scraping their peas back into the pot. "Okay. I'll count them all again. Jacob, you do *not* have two more than she does," she said in the convincingly calm voice she must use for negotiating an important contract.

I sat watching this performance, wondering how exactly it is that a person can go from well-respected business-woman to gritted-teeth lunatic trying to count peas out equally. But we've all been there. Of course, just as you're about to throw the whole lot in the bin, your beloved swans in (from his far more important career) to screams of "Daddy's home!" Miscalculated peas forgotten, the kids are happy, and you take a swig of cooking wine straight from the bottle.

– 4 –

Accidents will happen

You might remember a parenting book called *Siblings without Rivalry* that was a huge bestseller in the mid-nineties. I heard the author talking one day on *Oprah* or some other chat show on the telly. It caught my attention, sitting there with a tower of laundry at my feet, my pyjamas still on at four in the afternoon. I turned the volume up, straining to hear over the constant thumping and yelling going on upstairs. The house shook as someone was thrown against a wall. "Muuum!" one of them called for the billionth time. Convinced that this parenting guru had the Answer, I grabbed a coloured marker off the floor (feeling as if I'd won a free holiday simply because it wasn't dried up), and scribbled the name of the book on a used tissue.

I raced to the phone and called my local bookstore to inquire. "There's only one left in stock," a most understanding voice on the other end informed me. "Hold it!" I screamed.

"Get in the car! We're going to McDonald's!" I shouted to the boys. (Low blow, yes, but it was the best way to get my boys to put their shoes on in seconds.)

"If you can behave—and no hitting!—Mummy promises we can go on the slide and get a toy," I told them, knowing full well they couldn't last three minutes without pinching or shoving. "Mummy just has to buy a book first."

By the time the book was paid for, lumps of hair were already in someone's fist, and we were back in the car headed (thankfully) for home. (Sometimes, I would think to myself, I really am a cunning genius. I should be working for an intelligence agency rather than painting people's homes and doing laundry!)

"You two watch television and have these cookies while Mummy reads her new book," I said, mentally patting myself on the back, thinking, *God, I'm good.* I settled in at the kitchen table and happily cracked the spine of *Siblings Without Rivalry.* Now, no disrespect to the authors, but by the time I got through the "Talk Calmly to Your Children" chapter, another blood-curdling scream—the billionth one that day—had reverberated around the house, and I was ready to throw the thing in the trash. I headed for the living room, book in hand, and found one of the boys using the other as a trampoline. *Siblings Without Rivalry,* it turned out, was a perfect shield to protect myself as I tried to separate them. Experts, of course, will tell parents they shouldn't hit their kids, but I've never heard anyone say anything about using a fat parenting book to bonk them on the bum as you chase them up the stairs.

Yet another how-to-be-a-better-parent book bites the dust.

When the boys were small, they were very close. I would check on them at night, and invariably Josh had crawled into bed with Max. They were usually sprawled on top of each other, fast asleep, layered with a variety of blankets and toys like a giant BLT. No matter how many times I returned Josh to his bed, he'd be back in with Max (or us) by morning. But when they hit six and seven, the punching began.

I found it all exhausting. I'd gone from having happy and inquisitive little lads—content as long as they had each other to play with—to these rambunctious bickering boys who couldn't walk or move like the rest of the human race. It is inconceivable, for instance, for a seven-year-old boy to simply walk down the stairs, arms at his side. No—he must leap and try to touch the ceiling, thump his filthy paws on the wall and rattle the banister off its posts. If a sibling passes him headed in the other direction, there is not a hope in hell they won't bump, push or pinch each other. (Obscenities will be thrown into the mix several years later.)

There's a chemistry in a family, not unlike that in a relationship or a business partnership. Alliances are forged and dissolved, connections discovered. Our boys swung constantly between claims that they were the very best of friends to screams of "Mum! You don't *understand*. He wrecked my Leeeego! I HATE him!" Peace could reign for days, even months, and then the war would erupt as we witnessed a mass of legs and arms rolling along the upstairs hallway amid unintelligible shouts about someone's soccer ball being stolen.

Trying to keep up with it would give me a splitting headache. I knew, of course, that the fighting was the result of both of the boys' growing independence and need to strut their stuff. You only have to watch a pair of puppies or bear cubs (on National Geographic TV, not in your backyard) to know that such tumbling and wrestling is normal. Still, it didn't make it any easier to take. Tears became my best trick for putting an end to the commotion. It worked perfectly. All I had to do was throw my head down on the kitchen table and wail loudly—silent whimpering didn't cut it. I'm not sure this works as well with girls, but with my boys, at least, it was a smashing success every time.

"Mummy? Why are you crying?" they'd ask innocently, as if they'd been quietly knitting in the corner moments before.

"Because Mummy wants to leave home and go live with a quiet family who don't FIGHT!"

"Oh, we were only playing. Come on, Max, let's go and get the GI Joes out."

Lucky for me, boys' fights are generally quite black and white: wham, bam and suddenly they're playing again. I have two young nieces, eight and nine years old, who live nearby, and their sibling explosions are a much more complicated affair. They circle each other with words, play on each other's weaknesses and are already building their repertoire of hurtful girlie weapons for the future.

One of my friends, who's the mother of three young girls, actually ended up buying a second car because their weekly pilgrimage to the cottage was unbearable with all three in the vehicle together. It's the same as when I was growing up with my sisters. Rainy days—which happened often in the north of England—were my mother's worst nightmare. Three girls in close quarters would always be guaranteed bedlam. Since she died at just fifty-four, I try not to think of her screaming, "You girls will put me into an early grave!" (That's one threat I've never thrown at my kids—for purely selfish reasons.)

The fighting got so bad between Josh and Max that Hans and I decided we had to move one child out of their shared room. Just getting to their beds had become an obstacle course worthy of a *Survivor* challenge. Ropes swung from the light fixture, toy pieces were strewn about like land mines, and they'd dragged a chest of drawers and two of my best dining room chairs between their beds to act like the Berlin Wall. If either one crossed onto the other's territory he was dead meat. But of course I'm the one with the lasting scars—on my feet. My poor toes are misshapen and ugly, not because of tottering on too-high heels for the past twenty-five years but as a direct result of stumbling constantly on the razor-sharp Batmobile and Transformer bits that littered the floor of our house for more than a decade.

The Wall had to come down. It was not a happy day in our household, but it was the worst for Josh, whose new room was the old junk closet. Max, of course, was ecstatic when he realized he had a kingdom to call his own.

Poor Josh always hated his new room, and even today—towering over us—he doesn't much like to be by himself. When he's home, his bedroom door is always open and everything's in its right place: spread all over the floor. For years, before he went to sleep he would ask me to smooth out what he called the "worms" in his bed—little wrinkles on the sheets. After ten minutes of patting and smoothing, I'd stumble downstairs in search of the gin bottle and hear "Mummy, I've found another one!"

When they finally fall sleep, your kids look so peaceful and sweet that you almost forget they were driving you insane at bedtime. Even today, I love to wander in and stroke the boys' hair on the rare nights they're in bed before me. It was slightly embarrassing when I tried this recently. Josh was home from college and I snuck in, thinking he was sound asleep. A girl's head popped up: "Night, Ms. T!"

Where was that gin again?

Finding Mary Poppins

When my boys were little, and the painting business was getting busier, we went through every kind of nanny, babysitter and housekeeper. The nanny-cam had yet to be invented, but if I were to do it over again, I would definitely spy on the goings-on in our house with one of those carefully hidden cameras.

Still, even without that technology, I knew pretty well what went on in my house—it's called gut instinct. And if the children told me something about the babysitter, it was a pretty good bet that there was some truth in it. One Sunday morning after Hans and I had had a rare night out—leaving the boys with a rather attractive sixteen-year-old wannabe beauty queen—they simulated a sexual position that would have made the *Kama Sutra* proud. "That's what the babysitter did with her boyfriend," they explained—the one who'd apparently come around as soon as we pulled out of the driveway. Then there was the lovely Bajun lady who took hours to fold one basket of laundry, never did find the vacuum and ate most of Sunday's roast. There was also the unfortunate babysitter who took the kids to the petting zoo at a local park and had the end of her finger chewed off by a miniature wallaby.

After Elvy left us for another mother from the playground who doubled her salary (never boast about how wonderful your nanny is!), we ended up putting an ad in the local paper, hoping to find someone who was smart and had some common sense, though not necessarily experienced with kids. A Swedish scientist who happened to be studying children's behaviour for a paper she was writing applied for the job. She fitted the part perfectly. She was ramrod straight and looked like my old high-school headmistress with bosoms that could suffocate a small child. The kids were shipshape for the entire first week. But on the Friday I headed home earlier then usual, and found her standing at the bus stop down the street from our house. I pulled over and, feeling panicky, said, "Mrs. Leverhosen, where are the boys?" They're fine, she told me. She'd left them at home alone watching television. She was "decompressing," she explained. We never saw her again.

It's not easy finding Mary Poppins, and if you do you must count yourself very lucky. The trick is to keep quiet about her brilliance. Show off to other mothers and it's guaranteed that she will be swiped from under your nose by promises of a fabulous salary, Caribbean holidays and visas for all her relatives.

I finally found my vision of "super" nanny for my boisterous family in Lubov. You'd have been forgiven if you didn't realize at first glance that she was a woman. Lubov was a dream for our two active boys. She played soccer better than any of the dads on the Saturday-morning team (which she soon joined), and became the games leader in the local park. All the nannies would rush to her when she arrived with the boys because she was able to organize the neighbourhood children and keep them happy and busy for hours. I was the envy of the street. (You find Mary Poppins in the strangest places!) Surprisingly, she was even enthusiastic about housework, and had the uncanny ability to throw a baseball and wash the kitchen floor at the same time. For a couple of years—until we figured out our Russian dynamo was in the country illegally and she had to leave us—Lubov ran our house (and even built a small one in the backyard for herself out of shipping crates).

I was thrilled to have someone I could rely on to watch the boys, because I was frantically busy. There was more work than I could handle, and it had begun to take me out of town, to New York City and elsewhere. In fact, so many of my clients and other designers were asking me to teach them the art of paint effects—or faux finishing, as it became known—that I decided to open up a workshop. Overnight I was booked solid.

The only problem was that it was exhausting and I could only teach a handful of students at a time. Then I came up with a brainwave: how-to videos on everything from exercise and cooking to fly-fishing were huge. Why not a video on how to paint your walls like a Parisian boudoir or a Mexican cabana? I already knew how to produce television shows, so I figured I could shoot my own video. Over the next year I filmed three. They didn't have the highest production values of all time—I had little money and had to rope in friends to help out—but people bought them. In fact, all three became overnight successes, with some 250,000 copies sold. I'd hit a home run my first time.

You can still find *Decorative Painting Made Easy* 1, 2, and 3 out there somewhere—probably in your local library. If you want a really good laugh, have a look at it. I was terrible. Apart from appearing in commercials when I was modelling—when I was usually looking dreamily into the lens eating a chocolate biscuit, saying, "Mmmmmm"—these videos were my first experience on camera. Amazingly, the people who bought them didn't seem to care a bit about my performance. They were just glad that for next to nothing they could learn a craft that would make their home beautiful—with the bonus of having a weekend alone to paint while Dad kept the kids occupied.

Calls flooded in from researchers and producers wanting

to feature me and my work in magazines, newspapers and on talk shows. I had never been interviewed before, but I learned quickly how to handle each one differently: a business magazine would be after an entrepreneurial angle; a newspaper's home section wanted a decorating focus. I also discovered how weird it is to be interviewed. You can gauge the mood of the journalist or host immediately. The lady with the long skirts, Jesus sandals and hairy legs who plonked herself down and announced that she "only covers serious stories" (but was thrown into this one because someone was sick) really filled me with confidence.

"I'm sorry, Ms. Travis, I just don't get it—why would *anyone* want to spend their spare time rubbing a sponge soaked in paint over their living room walls?"

"It's fun! And creative and cheap!" I wailed. (That article went straight in the trash!)

The worst, though, was my very first radio interview. I generally love the immediate thrill of live radio (despite the fact that most of the hosts I've encountered are male, and their interest level in stencilling garlands around their kitchen walls is, well, nil), mostly because you don't have to brush your hair or even get out of your pyjamas, since interviews are often recorded from home.

This one, though, was at a local station with a well-known fixture on the radio scene, and I had to go to the studio. When I arrived, all fresh and excited, he had his feet up on the desk and was reading the sports page, a copy of the video beside him. "Well, well, ladies and gentlemen, what do we have here?" he blustered once we were on air. "There's this girl in my studio, Debbie Travis, and she's produced a little video about some new hobby called paint effects. Now that sounds about as boring as watching paint dry, huh, Debbie?" he guffawed at his own hilarious joke, and I began to cry. I spluttered and gulped my way through the first five minutes, explaining the history of paint finishes, when all of a sudden he began to look confused. There was a large box on the table beside us with a mass of buttons—all of them flashing. The controller knocked frantically on the window, "Start taking calls! The lines are blocked." (The host recently invited me back on his show to talk about my eighth book on the subject of paint. I gracefully declined.)

It was on the television talk shows, though, that I really learned how to make something as boring as painting into the next big thing. It was the time before decorating shows (even Martha had yet to become *Martha*), and there were daytime lifestyle programs that usually had both a male and a female host. He would demonstrate the new innovation in garden tools, and she would take care of cooking, decorating and crafts. They were always bubbly but usually bored stiff filming the same old stuff five days a week. Because I was something new, there always seemed to be a buzz in the air when I was on.

It was chaos for me as I tried to prepare the demos at home, then drive or fly with a suitcase full of toxic materials and enough sharp weapons to arm a small battalion. (There's not a chance I could get away with it today—my pulley packed with inflammable glazes, a hammer, wood chisel and several razor blades would cause an international incident at the airport.) I would pre-paint boards to look like different stages in the process, preparing for a lasagna-style presentation. Step one, step two and—with the magic of television—voilà! Ancient stone blocks perfect for your suburban home in Dallas. As my confidence grew, so did my repertoire. I showed eager homeowners how to decorate everything from birdhouses to glittery toilet seats. They loved it all.

My children loved it, too. They would often help me get ready. The most fun were the Christmas-themed shows, but there was one that nearly turned into a disaster. I was a regular guest on a popular daytime program called *The Dini Petty Show* out of Toronto. It was live, with a large studio audience. My plan for the Christmas program was to demonstrate how to make your own Styrofoam trees festooned with jelly beans (very sophisticated stuff!) as a decorative alternative to candies in a bowl.

Before we went on, I'd enlisted the kids' help, spreading everything we needed out over our kitchen floor. We had thousands of toothpicks, miniature terra-cotta pots, cone-shaped Styrofoam and bags of jelly beans. The boys were in heaven, and with mouths jammed with sweets, we stuck the colourful candies on toothpicks, then into the cones. Each cone was about a foot high, and the idea was to have about ten finished to show the audience. But the jelly beans kept falling off, and I knew it had to be a tight mass of colour to look festive and fabulous. Intent on getting them to stick,

I used a glue gun, spray glue and then several coats of shiny varnish to give it a professional polish. By the time they were finished we could have sold them at Pottery Barn, but they were only decorative.

It was a school holiday, so the three of us loaded our trees into the car and drove off to the set. My small boys chatted to people backstage and were even given front-row seats. The demonstration was a big success. But horror of horrors, as I was standing onstage in the full glare of lights and camera, I saw the stagehands passing the finished trees—the ones with several layers of glue and varnish— around the audience as if they were hors d'oeuvres to be sampled. The children sat in the front row, wide-eyed, aghast. I shot them the Look—*Don't say a word!*

With the audience full of retirees, I'm pretty sure we had a few sets of cracked dentures that day. But, thankfully, nobody died (I imagine I wouldn't have been invited back), and the boys and I giggled as we raced out of there and down the highway. "Mummy, I'm going to tell my grandchildren this story someday," Josh piped up from the back seat. I wept with happiness most of the way home—now, that's bonding!

Thanks to the success of the how-to video, I was soon offered my own show. *The Painted House* began as thirteen simple episodes on how to transform just about any surface in your home using different paint effects. Looking back at these old shows, you might think the crew and I were tripping—or at least smoking something very strong—but it was really just an abundance of enthusiasm.

The Painted House was the first show of its kind in North America. One entire episode would be painting the tiniest entrance hall: there'd be a painted sky on the ceiling, gold leaf on the mouldings, a ragged wall, tortoiseshell baseboards and a marbleized console table with a decorated lamp. It sounds frightful now, but the show hit a chord and became an instant, worldwide success.

In the beginning, I was an appalling on-camera host. I'd become quite confident in front of a live audience on the talk shows, but shooting in someone's house, the crew and the homeowners all around, everyone watching me, was nerve-racking. I had a teleprompter to read my lines— something I insisted on (to the frustration of my crew). "Pick up the brush," I'd say, my eyes tracking the words across the screen. "Then stir the, uh, paint." It took a while for me to realize that if I was natural and talked the way I talk to any-one, just chatting, it would be so much better.

We filmed the first season of *The Painted House* in 1995. When we wrapped it up in 2002, we'd created nearly two hundred episodes—fourteen seasons in total. But the real suc-cess was that Hans and I, not the network, owned the show. We sold it and spun it into books, newspaper columns and eventually a product line (this, thanks to the genius of my old man). The show is still in rerun heaven, and I receive letters from people all over the world who've watched it and loved it. At this very moment, there's a mum in some corner of the world on her hands and knees painting a tartan pattern on her kitchen floor as she follows along with me on *The Painted*

House. It doesn't seem to matter where people live or what language they speak, the message *If I can do it, so can you* gets through to them. It's a warm, fuzzy feeling for me.

It was during that first season that Hans and I started working together for the first time. He was directing, and I was hosting and producing the show. In fact, when we started we had such a tiny budget that we were doing just about everything. As I made the kids their lunches early in the morning, I was also attempting to make some form of a meal for the crew. To put it in perspective, we had about $10,000 an episode at our disposal for *The Painted House*, about the same amount we spent on catering alone years later when *From the Ground Up* came along, my big-budget network series.

Anyone who has started her own business knows it lives and dies on pure hard work, little sleep and that constant knot in your stomach wondering if you can pay everyone at the end of the week. The toughest challenge for me was the naysayers. When we finished editing the first episode of *The Painted House*, I proudly showed it to a friend from North Carolina. "It's okay," she said. "But I doubt Americans would ever be interested in watching a television show about decorating." Of course she couldn't have been more wrong. We sold the series to PBS, our first American broadcaster, two weeks later. And now there are entire networks on the subject.

I never had time for the doubting Thomases. It's when you're under pressure that you figure out who your real friends are. Mine were invaluable to me then and still are today.

We shot that first series over three very hot weeks in the middle of the summer. I was clueless about what I was going to do with the kids because I dreaded leaving them with a babysitter, and the local day camps finished way too early. I was saved by my friend Roshi. "I have an idea," she said. "Let's hire three university students and make our own camp in my backyard. The kids can bring their own lunch and use the loo off the garage. As long as they stay out of my house, they can have the whole garden to play in." Which is exactly what we did. Those students took them on trips and to the park, and the rest of the time they swam in Roshi's big pool (hanging out in the garage if it was raining) and had the best summer ever. Everyone was happy.

That first summer was a real test of whether Hans and I could work together. Luckily it went well. I think the thing that has saved us—then and now—is that we are such opposites. I'm emotional and get madly into the details, and I develop strong connections to the people we work with and live to get my hands dirty. Hans is easygoing, much more reserved and matter-of-fact. If someone isn't doing the job, he'll just tell the person to go, whereas I'll get into the emotional side of it: "But she just lost her great-uncle on her mother's side, she's been having this pain in her ankle and her fish is sick. . . ." It's a good mix of different skills (though mine are better!).

There is no question you have to have 100 per cent trust in the other person. And a willingness to live and breathe your work. For us, it's turned out fine because we have the same goals: a close family, an interesting life and spending time together. (Though twenty-four hours a day can get rather ugly.) It does make for some interesting scenes for our film crew and office staff. Having an argument at work with Hans is not like disagreeing with another colleague—everything's on the table.

"No, I won't redo it. I hate you!" I'll scream. "Just for that, no dinner or sex for a month!"

"What else is new?" he'll mumble and walk away.

The Domestic Pressure Cooker

With our work getting more and more intense, Hans and I had to learn to juggle—quickly. But it was never easy, especially with two boys who never seemed to sit still. In fact, for most of his life, Josh could barely walk across a room without falling. If there happened to be a bowl of pasta near him, it would end up on the floor. He's broken every window in the house—either with a ball or going through it himself. He doesn't mean to do these things, he's just the clumsiest child. His knees are permanently scarred; the number of bones he's broken must be in the record books. It's certainly in the records at our local emergency department where we're on a first-name basis with the staff.

But Josh has always been polite and likeable, which somehow diffuses the drama. "Sorry to bother you, Mum," he'll say, calling from the phone in the library. "I slipped in the park and my foot is all floppy." "Mum? My finger seems to be sticking out in the weirdest direction," he'll mention quietly in the middle of dinner.

In the early days of *The Painted House,* we were shooting a promotional piece for PBS, and all the stuffy executives had come in from Boston to make sure I did it right. We couldn't afford a studio, so we filmed it in one of the children's bedrooms. The boys had actually become quite used to arriving home and finding the walls in their rooms had gone from looking like a painted meadow to resembling a panel of denim. But I was still new to hosting and quite nervous around these big executives. I told the kids that when they got home from school they could wave at me to say hi, but were then to go immediately to the basement and be quiet. (Well, a girl can dream . . .)

There I was, cameras rolling, smiling wonderfully and painting the walls in some fancy finish when I saw Josh gesturing to me in the doorway behind a sea of big execs. I was furious. He was doing this crazy pantomime, his hands in the air, as I tried my hardest to ignore him. "I've broken my thumb playing basketball," he mouthed. "What should I do?"

Without missing a beat or a brush stroke, smile still plastered on my face, I said, "Get the bus to emergency. I'll follow later."

I completely forgot about him in the chaos of the day (Mother of the Year, I know!), but Hans was called by the hospital half an hour later. "Uh, sir, we have a boy here who says you're his father. Do you mind coming and getting him?"

If that sort of thing happened to someone on one of my sets now, I'd just say, "No problem, we'll take a coffee break while you sort it out." But when you're just starting out in a business, it's hard to make that call. You think those bigwigs are just going to drop you because your kid needs your attention for a second.

Eventually, I came to expect such interruptions. That finger was only one of Josh's many calamities. He has a small strip of metal in his leg where he was crushed playing rugby. He also broke his arm in England in a pub, but the craziest was breaking his foot in the library.

One afternoon, I received a call from our ancient librarian, a once-sweet old lady who loved her job. (The groups of boys who ran through "her" library at every opportunity drove her to distraction, I'm sure.) "Ms. Travis," she bellowed, her library whisper all but forgotten, "Joshua has broken his foot and is presently lying on my desk unable to move."

"How did he do *that* in the library?" I said in as threatening a tone as I could muster, but with the usual sense of dread that it would turn out to be his fault.

"He was chasing his brother along the top shelves and slipped on a copy of *A Christmas Carol.* Seems he plummeted down eight shelves and landed on the hamster cage."

I was so shocked that I never did ask the condition of the hamster.

Broken arms and feet are serious, of course, but active kids suffer lots of minor injuries, too. My mum had a great trick to help kids deal with the pain. If we scrapped a knee or stubbed a toe or fell off our bikes, she'd say, "Looks like you need a Shock Pill." And she'd pull out this little tin of homeopathic tablets—tiny little round dots made from camomile or something gentle—and she'd tell us to put the pill under our tongue and wait for it to dissolve. I did the same with my boys. It had to be something sweet, but not a recognizable candy (since then it loses its magical power). The idea behind this trick is that when they have it under their tongues, they can't cry or carry on. By the time the Shock Pill dissolves, the hurt is gone, too.

I still think of those years as the age of accidents. I would come home at night and brace myself to hear who had been hurt, which kid had punched the other and how our poor house had suffered in the process. It was a difficult time—one of the hardest. It reached a peak one evening when Hans announced he would rather I didn't bombard him with all the family mess as soon as he walked in the door. He needed time to decompress after his day. The room went deathly silent, like the calm before a big storm. Then the hurricane hit. When the dust had settled and the furniture had been pushed back into place, he agreed he'd never say *that* again!

I needed time to decompress, too. Some days I'd come in the house and go directly to the sink and start peeling potatoes. It didn't matter that no one wanted them. It was my chance to move from my work life into being a mum. All this bedlam would be happening around me and I would just zone out on my potatoes.

It can be incredibly hard to juggle all the different parts of your life. When things get really insane at work and home, I have a tendency to panic. Going around with a thousand problems in my head, the pressure of our employees' livelihoods resting on my shoulders, I'm not surprised that I can never find the car keys or remember how to work the bloody remote, and insult the dishwasher repairman for being two minutes late. Women often ask me who "did" my nose, but the truth is my up-tilted snoot is not the result of surgery, it's from constantly rubbing my hand up my face in desperation.

Luckily, Hans always (well, nearly always) stays calm. He's the kind of man who has the boys' lunches made and packed by 8 a.m. and leaves the kitchen spotless after a chaotic evening at home. I'm slumped in a chair with a bottle of something strong, while he's loading the dishwasher, humming, a towel hung jauntily over his shoulder.

When Hans is away, our house literally falls apart. I have heard of people who can't wear a watch because the minute they put it on, the watch stops. Our house is like that when Hans leaves: it just stops functioning, everything breaks, there are floods and leaks. The place is a total disaster: the piles of clothes, dishes and papers grow like an alien mass.

The only problem is that being so calm, he's a terrible person to argue with. He simply won't fight back. Still, over twenty years we've had a handful of doozies, and it's guaranteed that the kids remember every one in gory detail—lest *we* forget. The argument the boys most love to dredge up and remind me about occurred when I threw a cup at Hans's head. It bounced off him and hit the kitchen wall that I had just painted in the most beautiful colour wash. I was furious. The wall was impossible to repair without looking as if it had been patched. I didn't care if their father had a giant goose egg on his forehead, he'd ruined my paint finish!

The trick to managing through all this chaos is having that core line of love. Of course, we're all constantly flipping on either side of the line. (When Hans was away recently, I missed him like a lovesick teenager. He knew better, and said, "Wait until I get home, you'll want to be rid of me." He was right, of course.) Family life is like the tail of a fish flapping around—you adore them one minute, you want to run screaming from them the next, but love is the constant.

There were days when I was producing and hosting and running an ever-expanding office that I felt completely overloaded. Life was much too much. I would stop in my tracks and have no idea what I'd been doing the minute before. At home it felt as if I was in a domestic pressure cooker.

But then suddenly it clicked. All the problems and questions I had to deal with are what life's all about. I wasn't going to arrive one day at some perfect moment when everything would be just right. I will always be working at it, finding solutions that make sense in that hour, in that day, that week. But there will *always* be solutions—and when you find one (even when it's a little thing like getting your eight-year-old to make his bed without asking a billion times) you feel creative and strong. The problem might still be there (and it will likely rear its ugly head again) but the intensity has abated.

I have a friend who spent every day after school from three to seven in the evening picking up and dropping off her four kids at a variety of after-school programs. She was a miserable basket case. The solution, of course, was to stop. It seemed impossible until one night she gathered the whole family together and talked to them. Turned out all but one of the kids didn't care if they played trumpet or did ballet or whatever they were doing. Now they spend evenings together as a family. So Johnny doesn't become a world-class trumpet player. He probably wouldn't have anyway—even if his mum *was* devoting her life to racing around like a maniac, battling traffic to get him to the conservatory three times a week. The truth is, kids are likely to have better memories of playing Scrabble with their family, anyway.

Of course I'm not talking about big answers, all-encompassing solutions, and I'm not referring here to people who are struggling with poverty or divorce, illness or the death of someone they love, because that's a different story altogether. But for the rest of us who are pushing through working and raising a family, dealing with the many ups and downs, problems are just part of living.

You might even find the solution is in changing your own attitude: having a rest, talking to a friend, spending some time on your own. Mothers tend to believe that the world is going to stop if they take a break or let down their guard for a minute—even if they just ask for help. So many of us have been brought up by generations of women who put themselves last. My own mother died the year her last child left home. She was never able to enjoy her grandchildren or let us look after her. She rarely took the time to eat properly, never exercised (except for running after us) and certainly never had the luxury of time to herself. (I like to imagine her reaction to a modern yoga class. "Thank yourself for taking the time to focus on your breath"? She would have roared with laughter. Puuuleeze!)

You have to put yourself on par with the other most important aspects of your life: your children, your marriage and your work. Women who forget to pay attention to their own needs either snap or end up on the other end of parenting—the empty nest—with nothing in common with their husbands and no recollection of the qualities that made them passionate before all those poopy diapers and scraped knees. It's not selfish to look after yourself, it's imperative.

My friend Christine, a busy real estate agent and mother of three, was so frazzled and exhausted recently that she stole away for the afternoon and treated herself to a massage and pedicure at a cushy spa. She was sitting in the lounge, blissed out, wearing her big fluffy white robe, drinking herbal tea, when she spotted her cleaning lady, also the mother of two, in *her* fluffy robe relaxing in a chair nearby. They laughed and had a glass of wine together. Two tired mums.

Everyone needs a break sometimes. It's as I always say: happy mummy, happy home!

Kids need to be competitive. It's a natural part of growing up—but do their mothers have to be so cutthroat? Picking up your children at school, listening to them tell their stories should be a joy. Instead you find yourself wondering if you're up to scratch—maybe you should have had your hair blow-dried, or the car washed, maybe waxed—the legs, as well. It's silly, of course, but it's not easy to keep your self-esteem in place with Yummy Mummies patrolling the playground like exotic birds of prey.

The drive home isn't much better as the kids reel with excitement over the upcoming birthday party where Hannah Montana will be performing (with Jamie Oliver on the food). A feeling of dread engulfs you as you sit in your ancient car surrounded by chip bags and empty juice cartons, the vague smell of decomposing takeout in the air. The birthday picnic in the park you were organizing is starting to seem . . . well, pathetic—and you were going to go all out with a pirate theme and treasure hunt! Even the eye patches you'd planned to make out of knicker elastic and felt seem lame after the loot bag packed with an iPod and Cirque du Soleil tickets that your daughter came home with last week. Come on, you think, you're a grown woman with a busy, interesting life of your own—you don't have to compete with these supermummies. Still, maybe you could try a wee bit harder . . . give up the sweats and flip-flops for school pickup tomorrow? *Oh my God, is she wearing Manolos in the sandbox?*

– 5 –

Yummy mummy and other playground species

Going to school for the first time can be as traumatic for mothers as it is for kids. It sometimes feels a bit like high school, with the other parents checking you out (as you are them), the playground dividing into camps. From this day onward you know you'll be seeing this group of parents more than your closest friends (the ones you *chose* because you actually like them).

Of course, school can be a wonderful place to meet people from different backgrounds and cultures. Where else are you going to be drawn together with such a disparate crew, the only shared identity being parents? (It's guaranteed that your kid will become best buddies with a child from a family so different from your own that they might as well be from another planet.)

Some of those parents will become your support system, people you can rely on to help out when you're in a pinch;

others will turn into real friends long after the kids leave home. Some won't. But most of us make an effort to get along—partly for the kids' sake and partly because you're likely to be forced together for years to come.

My boys went to the same school from the age of five to eighteen. They were known as "lifers." I chose the school not because it's the best but because it's the nearest—right across the road. Rule number one in my books: make life as easy as possible. The school bell was our morning alarm clock. "Hurry! The bell's gone—get out of bed! Quick! *Of course* Pop Tarts are healthy. Yes, I've finished your essay. Have a lovely day!" was our morning mantra.

It didn't take long for me to be able to decipher the different traits of the various playground species. The Yummy Mummy—always friendly, slim of leg and dressed in either full tennis regalia or the latest Gucci or Pucci—is probably the easiest to spot. You're just glad you got out of the house with your child in matching shoes, his clothes without holes (mostly) and a face that passes for clean, and you try not to gawk as she slips effortlessly out of her Range Rover and plants a perfectly lip-glossed kiss on her pristine six-year-old.

The Yummy Mummy is always busy. Her days are packed with hours at the gym, lunch, tennis and massage. She tops it off with picking up the kids at school, nanny in tow (I never have been clear on why a person would need help if she's already going to collect her kids—does she need a reminder of their names?).

I'm jealous, naturally. I'm generally in a state of wardrobe malfunction. When you're constantly in a mad rush with an ever-growing list swimming in your brain, the art of perfect grooming is particularly elusive. Last week I sat on the edge of the boardroom table in our offices, legs swinging, chatting to my team about the successful design event we'd held the night before. As I looked down, I noticed a huge bulge on my right calf. As I rattled on to the group about what an amazing job they had all done, I casually shoved my hand up my pant leg and pulled out the offending lump. It was the previous night's knickers. I laughed it off, though the style interns sitting in the front row could barely contain their horror.

It's all about how you fill your day. What's important to one person—massage? yoga class?—is a mundane chore to another, a luxury to someone else. I remember once being called into the school for a parent meeting. I'd completely forgotten about it until one of the kids angrily phoned to remind me. I was filming at the time and was in the middle of a demonstration on how to transform an ugly concrete mantel into sophisticated granite (using only a can of paint, of course). Dropping everything, I raced to the school, still in my overalls, paint in my hair. As I rushed into the building, I bumped into another mother who looked just as stressed. "Hi, Debbie," she sighed. "You look as crazed as I feel."

"God, tell me about it," I said, calming down a wee bit, relieved to find someone similarly frenzied.

"Yeah, what a day I've had. Do you know my manicurist has cancelled on me twice today? And now, with this meeting, I have to reschedule my massage. What we do for our kids!'"

I stared at her, gobsmacked, fantasies of violence playing in my head—should I gouge her eyes out with my bare hands or apply a quick karate chop to the neck? Instead, I sat in the meeting, wondering if *I* was the one who had it all wrong. Maybe my kids would be better off if my greatest stress was my unmanicured nails. (There is nothing like other mothers for planting the seed of self-doubt.)

But even though the Yummy Mummies make the rest of us feel hopelessly dishevelled and slightly homicidal, it's the Domestic Divas who truly put everyone to shame. They are like throwbacks to the 1950s housewife, but without the immaculate grooming. They're at every baseball game, seated in fold-up chairs (their child's name and jersey number hand-embroidered on the back), cheering on their kids (and ours), nourishing snacks at the ready— enough for the entire team. Their backpacks are filled with first-aid kits that would put a tropical missionary to shame, plus all the right toys to keep the younger kids busy.

I was recently talking to my two grown lads, fondly remembering those sunny afternoons when I cheered them on from the sidelines, standing my ground beside the Domestic Divas. While I recalled hustling to get them there and patting them cheerily on the back when they scored a goal, they offered a slightly different version of events.

"You always took us to the wrong pitch, we were usually late and you never brought water, never mind anything to eat," Max said.

"Yeah, we were always starving after school and had to beg other mothers for food," Josh chimed in.

"I was there, wasn't I?" I shot back.

Max gave me a bracing scowl. "Yeah, but you were so busy chatting that you never watched the game." (That is *so* not how I remember it.)

The Domestic Diva runs her household with the organizational skills of a general. The mudroom is her barracks: there are hooks with each child's name stencilled above, and, yes, there are actually coats hanging on them; baskets and containers are filled with folded scarves, hats and there's not a mismatched pair of gloves in sight; there are even baby wipes by the back door to wipe down muddy feet and paws. Her dishwasher is always empty, there are no takeout cartons on the counter from last night, and I can guarantee the beds are made with hospital corners.

But the scariest part of the Domestic Diva's home is the daily activity chart in the kitchen neatly filled in with multicoloured markers, every minute of each day accounted for (no writing of "don't forget hockey at 3 p.m. on the palm of *her* hand). After-school programs that run the gamut from Suzuki violin lessons and gymnastics for miniature Olympic hopefuls to pottery for the potty trained are all listed in detail.

I just feel slouchy around these moms—they must do *something* wrong, maybe drinking in secret in the broom closet during the afternoon?

But the scariest mummy of all has to be the Volunteer Vulture. We all know the type. You're loitering in the hallway at pickup time, when the principal asks if anyone would be so kind as to accompany the teachers and class for apple picking this Friday. The Volunteer Vulture appears out of nowhere, arms waving madly.

"Yes, wonderful, Ms. Brown—again. Anyone else?" the principal asks, straining to catch your eye as you hide behind your cardboard cup of stale school coffee. (The teachers always seem to know who hasn't done their bit—you can sense your position on their eternal list of shame.)

If I did get dragged along on the class trip, I was sure to link up with a couple of mums I liked in order to have a good natter. The key was that as soon as we got off the school bus (if you've never been a passenger on one, I heartily recommend it—so much fun on your hemorrhoids), we'd head for the museum coffee shop and leave the teacher and the Volunteer Vulture to bounce through the butterfly exhibition. You can be sure that during dinner the Vulture will be regaling her family with her knowledge of every moth in the place.

Of course, there are amazing volunteers who unstintingly provide the extra help needed by every school these days. They work incredibly hard, and my admiration goes out to them. But for those of us who also have busy and demanding work, it's not easy to either make the time or be patient with the endless meetings and chitchat that are par for the course in organizing school events.

For years I was probably one of the worst culprits in the volunteer-shirking department, but finally the pressure built up and I guiltily offered my services for Lasagna Day. (I know I heard a gasp and a few giggles from the Volunteer Vultures when I stuck up my hand. *"Well, that's a first!"*)

Lasagna Day was a major fundraiser at my boys' school. Working over a weekend, parents and teachers made several thousand lasagnas, which were frozen and then sold for an exorbitant rate (no parent dares buy fewer than ten), making a ton of money for the school.

Saturday morning, my apron on, feeling very pleased with myself, I strutted across to the school. The kids waved proudly from the doorway; Hans shouted, "Try and behave!" from behind them. "Christ," I called over my shoulder, "I can make a lasagna in my sleep!"

When I arrived, the gym was set up like an assembly line, the whole thing run by the Queen of the Volunteer Vultures, Know-It-All Nancy (her résumé probably reads, "bossy but gets things done").

"Ms. Travis, you're late. Go and tuck yourself between Dr. Metcalfe and Betty. Quickly now."

Giggling like a six-year-old, I sidled up to my great friend Mike (who's the father of three boys and runs a busy emergency unit at a local hospital) and Betty, the art teacher, who happens to be a fan of mine. (I've stolen many of her great class projects for my TV shows.)

Nancy's crew had it down to a science. Each portion of cheese, each ladle of sauce had to be measured and weighed with the precision expected in a laboratory. The process was painfully slow. As a businesswoman running my own company I figured I could find some efficiencies, speed things up a bit, and the three of us started to do our own thing. Mike was on pasta, I was on sauce, Betty had cheese detail. We soon developed a production line that was knocking out lasagnas at record pace.

But when Nancy got word of our innovations, instead of a pat on the back we were given a stern warning and informed that we were to abandon our production line and follow her rigid instructions to the T. When she caught us still doing our routine half an hour later, she suggested in an angry whisper (which the entire gym and most of the street could hear) that perhaps Lasagna Day wasn't the best fundraiser for us.

"What's wrong?" I said, not willing to back down. "We've done forty and the others have only done three each!"

"But look at them. I can't sell *those*," she said.

They were a bit shabby, I agreed, but we were producing more than anyone else, and wasn't that the point? We had three thousand lasagnas to make!

"Come on!" I said. "Does it really matter if there's more cheese on some and the sides are a bit scruffy?"

That's when she totally lost it. "Matter? Yes, it matters!"

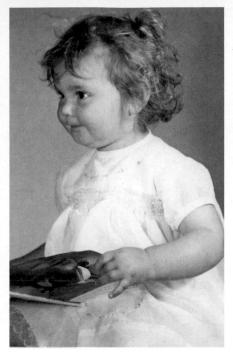

Me at seven months, already looking like trouble.

My parents, Val and Billy, in the late 1950s.

I stayed with my grandma in Monte Carlo when my father was ill, and went sailing on her friend's yacht.

My grandma in her thirties—always elegant.

On the cover of a British fashion magazine at 19.

So '80s. Me in a fashion spread in a Dutch magazine.

Hans, the proud dad of one-year-old Josh and a newborn Max.

Nothing like a toddler's sloppy kiss.

Max never took off his goggles for the whole two weeks in Spain.

Josh and Max playing in the rain.

The boys at the beginning of term all squeaky clean, which lasted a couple of days.

Josh makes the football team in Grade 7.

Max on holiday with us in Italy at 16.

I wore these overalls
for seven years on
The Painted House.

Me and my *Facelift* gang.

This is what it's all about.

And this, too: the boys and their dad.

The three sisters: me with Joanna and Emma.

Joanna with me and our baby brother, Will.

We built a house in seven weeks for my TV show *From The Ground Up*.

Hans's passion is his vintage motor bikes, and maybe me!

She was hopping around, her face red, eyes popping out of her head. "It does! It does!"

Finally, Mike and I were asked to leave. We got the boot. We were fired from Lasagna Day.

Volunteering can be a nightmare, but the insanity of parental politics probably reaches its pinnacle at the dreaded birthday party. For several years when your children are in school there is a party just about every bloody week, each one more elaborate than the next.

Max was one of those strange children who had to be forced into everything—especially parties. When he was young he would cry, begging us not to make him go. He would say he had no friends, that nobody liked him. "So why have you been invited?" I'd ask him kindly. We'd arrive at the party and have to drag him up the stairs hanging on to my ankles. Then I'd leave and cry all the way home, imagining my poor darling sitting by himself in the corner the whole time. Inevitably, when I went to pick him up he'd be desperate to stay. I'd have to pull him out the door.

"I hate you," he'd say. "You're always picking me up too early."

"But everyone else has left!"

Mothers go crazy trying to make these parties the best they can for their precious ones—though it's rarely enough for kids today, who, shuttled to hundreds every year, become birthday party connoisseurs. I proudly made my own cakes, and every year my sons would whine, "Pleeease can't we just have a cake from Dairy Queen like everyone else?" I was talking recently with a single mum who hosted what she thought was a fabulous sixth birthday for her son in the local park, complete with soccer and a picnic, pin the tail on the donkey—the whole works. One of the kids came up to her and said, "This is the worst party I've ever been to. It sucks."

When I was a child, we always had the coolest activity at my birthday every year. My parents would borrow a pony from the farmer down the road and offer my friends pony rides. It was the closest I was going to get to my childhood dream of having my own horse and being like Elizabeth Taylor in *National Velvet*. The pony was free because Dad knew the farmer, but it always raised my hopes about having my own horse because he was so enthusiastic about the day—that's until I realized he was just pleased to have the manure to fertilize his garden. In those days, the birthday girl always went last, so by the time my forty overeager classmates had a ride, the elderly pony was exhausted, dragging itself up and down our street. Still, I wouldn't have dared complain, or I'd have been sent to my room.

Of all the modern birthday madness, however, it is the loot bag that's the most outrageous. They were unheard of when I was a child in England, and I still fail to see the point of loading children up with dollar-store rubbish after you've just thrown a lovely party. They hover at the door like carrion birds hoping for their bag of future landfill. (On the other hand, there is nothing more humiliating than having your child trot home from someone else's fab party with a loot bag worth more than the $15 Transformer you shelled out for as a present—or even worse, a loot bag containing an even better Transformer than the one you gave.)

One year I put my foot down. No loot bags. I stood at the front door bravely explaining over and over again to stunned kids and shocked parents that I was starting a new trend and they were all leaving empty-handed. It began with a simple "Nope, no loot bags. Hope you had a brilliant time!" then "Sorry, no loot bag." By the time the last kid was glaring up at me, my knees were buckling with shame. "It's been such a terrible year for my husband's business you see. . . . We may have to sell the house." The next year we had loot bags stuffed full of enough crap to keep the Taiwanese economy buoyant for years to come.

As parents we're all in this crazy situation together. If only we could realize that we all have the same goal—surviving and raising kids who are healthy and happy—it would be a whole lot more pleasant for everyone.

Many of the battles, though, go back to the age-old tension between the working mum and the mother who chooses to stay at home. Both jobs are incredibly hard, occasionally rewarding and often mind-numbingly boring—it's a personal decision about how you want to live your life. When we look down our noses at someone else's choice, no one wins—bitchy remarks don't help much, either.

When *The Painted House* became a regular fixture on television, I was constantly recognized on the street. People were always kind and complimentary, but the other mothers could be divided into two camps. There were the "Wow, things look great, Debs. You must be madly busy. If I can help out with the kids, just let me know" mothers and the ones who had the guilt knife always at the ready. Once, while I was watching a kids' soccer match, a woman leaned over and expressed her deep concern.

"So how are the kids handling all this?" she asked, as if there had been a death in the family.

"What do you mean?" I said, utterly confused.

"Oh, you know, all the fame. You must never be home. Your poor children."

Those were the times when the British stiff upper lip came in handy.

It's too bad, because if mothers could just embrace one another, offer support instead of nastiness, we could probably take over the world—make things better for everyone.

On my street we have every type of mum. On one side of us there's crazy, wonderful Helen with her two kids and her work at the hospital; Lynn down the street has a mega-job at a cosmetics company and juggles three young girls; Andrea, around the corner, stays at home with her young son. There is also Bedra, a kind and beautiful woman from Lebanon who lives with her family in the basement of a larger home several houses up. She cleans other people's homes and is always offering to help out with babysitting. She needs the extra cash, though she always arrives with delicious Lebanese treats to share. Andrea bakes batches of cookies for everyone, and Lynn brings us amazing makeup samples from her work. Helen always has a corkscrew to hand. I'm the one with the decorating advice. We all have something to offer, and when we share a glass of wine together we laugh and cry at the same things. Every mother is hard-working—it comes with the territory. We're all hurtling down the same highway, hoping for the best.

Street Smarts

One of my heroes is Sir Richard Branson, the multi-millionaire Virgin tycoon. As an entrepreneur, he embraces every venture (and he's had many—from music to film, soft drinks to banks, even his own airline) with nonstop enthusiasm. He is one of Britain's and the world's great success stories. He was brought up in the 1950s, and his mother decided to set challenges for her children in order to make them independent. He often tells the story about when he was four years old and she stopped the family car several miles from their house, told him to find his way back and drove off. He was soon completely lost, but eventually made it home.

Tough love like that is extreme, but I'm sure the experience (and other ones she came up with), planted a seed of strength inside him. While I'm not saying parents should abandon their four-year-old in a field (they'd probably be arrested), I do feel passionately that we have swung too far in the opposite direction. By protecting them all the time and hovering over their every action, we're softening our children in a way that robs them of their tools for living.

It's rare to see kids hanging from tree branches in the park or on the street riding their bikes without parents or nannies—even in suburbia where it's supposed to be safer. I recently read a piece in a major American newspaper accompanied by a large photograph of an empty suburban street shot on a warm Sunday afternoon. The headline read, "Where have all the children gone?" I know where they've gone. They're inside playing video games because their parents think it's too "dangerous" outside.

We were once called into the boys' school for a parent talk about the perils of children and the Internet. I put my hand up and said, "I think kids are better off riding around on their own on their bikes than spending all their time on the Internet." I was flabbergasted that a good portion of the room thought I was wrong.

I think this kind of attitude is sad and is doing more harm than good to our kids. Have these parents forgotten their own childhood—and all the things they learned when they weren't hiding under their mother's skirt? I'm not saying we should turn the clock back, but all this molly-coddling and overprotectiveness means we're taking away the experiences that made *us* who we are.

When I was a child, my mother would scream, "Out!" at eight on a Saturday morning, and as long as I was home for tea at four o'clock I would avoid her wrath. One day, I met two tramps sitting on a fence by the field at the end of our road, and they asked me if I had any money for a pint. (I'm quite certain it was beer, not milk, that they had in mind.) I told them my father would give them a drink if they wanted to come home with me. I was nearly as scruffy after playing outside all day as they were, and I brought them home and sat them down in the kitchen. My mother walked in as I was serving them lemonade and cookies. I still have one ear that's slightly longer than the other thanks to the way she dragged me up to my room. The old guys were sent packing with a couple of ham sandwiches and a piece of fruitcake (my dinner).

Life was simpler then, of course, and there was less traffic. You can't really let your children run completely free in the city, but Hans and I did what we could, choosing to live in a very tight-knit downtown neighbourhood. Everything is within walking distance, the school is across the street, the park and a library are down the road. We knew we could have had a much grander house if we lived somewhere else, but we chose to stay because having everything so handy made balancing our work and family much easier, and our lives far more liveable. I always ask people who complain about commuting to work in the city if the trade-off—often a bigger home, a backyard—is worth it. You might have to live in a smaller place or have your kids play in the local park instead of on your lawn, but the daily grind could well be simpler, even better, without all that driving and rushing around just to get where you need to go.

Considering that we live in a busy city, the boys managed to have a rather memorable childhood running in the streets of our neighbourhood. We started off slowly: allowing them to walk up to the neighbour's house or to school with their friends. (Even if we had to follow them secretly the first few times to make sure they did as we told.) We figured that if we wanted them to take the subway or bus on their own when they were older, they had to start building their street smarts. (The chance that your kids will get accosted is minute, but the chance they'll become mushy-brained wimps is very, very high!)

Anne, a friend of mine who has also made it across the finish line with her two boys—eighteen and twenty-two—calls this approach "benign neglect." It's an attitude that says kids need space to explore the world without their parents hovering all the time. That's not to say there aren't rules and consequences, and firmness when necessary, but they should feel that they have responsibility for themselves, as well.

Of course, they will get into mischief—but they'll learn from that, too. Near where we live there's a lawn bowling club, one of these old English places with a pristine green lawn and superb old pensioners dressed in their traditional whites. Josh's favourite game was always (and still is) war manoeuvres. He and his friends would slither through the bushes on the edge of the lawn, then silently roll apples in between the bowling balls—to the great confusion of the old people. But it was the end of these antics when, instead of apples, they tossed in firecrackers.

I was having a rare quiet afternoon when the doorbell rang. I went to answer it and found a livid little white-haired man holding Josh and his friend Justin by their ears. He was furious. "You should lock them up!" he told me. "Ship them off to the army, the badly behaved brats!"

He was absolutely right, of course, but instead of the army Josh was made to mow their lawn for the next month. Now that he's studying the Second World War, my badly behaved brat is a pal of some of these war veterans, and it's the highlight of their week when he spends his evening listening to their tales of battle.

Mayhem and Meltdowns

My happiest mothering moments were those heady times when Mummy was always right. When your children are little, you can do no wrong. I could make up stories, tell the boys I'd been in the Olympics and they would just say, "Wow, Mummy, you're amazing." Until I wasn't anymore.

It starts sometime about seven or eight years old, when they're becoming more and more independent. First they begin to notice that other families do things differently. Josh came home one day after visiting a friend and asked me if we were really poor. "No," I said, "not this week."

"So why don't we have an elevator in our house?"

The next step is realizing their parents are flawed—and may even be quite embarrassing to them at times. After shopping one afternoon with the boys, I came home all charged up and was telling Hans all about it. "Honestly," I explained, "I got out of the car at Ikea and was mobbed—there must have been thousands of shoppers wanting my autograph!"

"No, Mum, there were three," Josh said. "And one lady just wanted to know if the sale had begun."

"You're being cheeky. Off to your room!"

"But you're telling lies."

"Don't question your mother," I said, my finger pointed up the stairs.

Moments like those you know intuitively that it's the beginning of the end—no longer your curly-topped, gullible angels, your children have their own opinions. Shame.

But even with all this newfound independence, I found that my boys also really needed one-on-one time. In fact, they craved it. Even if it was just a mundane chore—picking up light bulbs at the hardware store—it would be an exciting treat if one of them went alone with one of us. It made them feel special.

When the boys turned eight, I took each of them on a solo trip to New York. We stayed in relatively posh hotels and excitedly explored the city together. We walked up Fifth Avenue, took a calèche ride in the park and went to fancy restaurants for dinner. We talked like two middle-aged people and discussed life in general. Both trips are some of my happiest memories—seeing my little lad in his smart clothes (that soon changes!), legs dangling above the floor, trying to read a menu nearly as large as he is.

When it was Max's turn, we went to dinner at a well-known high-end place that was a huge treat for both of us. Max had dressed himself in a little bow tie and jacket. We were just getting settled when the waitress came over and started collecting Max's silverware. "Excuse me," I said. "What are you doing?"

"Kids steal it," she explained, as if he wasn't even in the room.

Those astonishing lioness instincts that lie dormant in every mother until her offspring is threatened sprang into action.

"Excuse me," I said to my youngest, smiling through gritted teeth. "I'll be back in a second."

I followed the snooty waitress around the corner and pinned her up against the kitchen wall. "You will return all the silverware to the table, and you will make that little boy feel like the most important gentleman in the room—which, for your information, he is—or tomorrow I will guarantee you will not have a job," I hissed in her ear (far more bravely than I felt).

The rest of the evening was magical, with samples of every dessert in the place offered for Max to try (on the house, of course). As we left, the waitress tapped me on the shoulder. "I am so sorry," she said.

That one-on-one time with my children changed the terms of our relationship, even if only subtly. It was a unique experience just the two of us shared, as well as a recognition of their growing independence. And it's as important for parents as it is for kids. When your children are eight and nine—and doing what is normal for that age, testing you, questioning you—it's easy to forget how much they truly look up to their parents. We are their role models. They never stop watching us and are incredible sponges. They're observing the dynamics between their mother and father, between their mother and her friends, how you talk about your life, even how you treat yourself.

I think often of the times my grandmother would come to visit us from the south of France and she and my mother would sit in our "best room"—a place we were not allowed to enter except on special occasions. We'd be allowed to curl up at their feet to listen to them hooting with laughter as they shared their stories. It's why talking to your children about your work, even about the hard times and how they affect you, is so important. They love our stories, and by watching us they are starting to write their own.

When I was working on *The Painted House,* I became very close to the crew. I always say that our people are our best resource, the key to our success. One day when the boys were about eight and nine, one of the cameramen with whom I'd travelled all over the world, who had a knack of making me look good from every camera angle (not an easy feat!), left us to go work on a big film in Los Angeles. Hans told me about it in the office.

"How could he?" I sobbed. I carried on for a while there, but was so upset that I ended up going home. I walked through the front door crying uncontrollably. I cried all the way through dinner. "Why did he leave us?" "What am I going to do without him?" et cetera, et cetera. Hans had his pull-yourself-together face on at that point, and the children just sat and stared.

"Why don't you go upstairs," Hans suggested.

I threw myself on the bed like an actress in an old black-and-white movie. But it was the boys coming into our bedroom, their wide eyes filled with concern, asking if everything was all right, that made me get my act together.

"Mummy's fine," I said, sniffling. "I'm just upset that Kevin doesn't want to work with me anymore."

I felt like a complete idiot as Josh went out and found me a tissue—"Mummy, your nose is running"—but ultimately, it was good for them to see me have a meltdown. Everyone has failures and times when they mess up or are deeply upset. Kids need to know that it's often those times when life doesn't work out as planned that you learn the most about how to manage situations in the future.

Seeing me have my very own tantrum also gave Josh and Max an opportunity to reverse our roles—something children love to do. Those moments when children turn the tables and comfort their parents are breathtaking: they show us that our children have the capacity to empathize. They also give us a glimpse at what kind of adult they may turn out to be.

"You are a great mum, and when we grow up we're going to be your cameramen," the sweet little boys told me that day. "It's going to be okay."

Even though I could barely breathe for crying, watching the boys pat my hand and comfort me, I knew that I'd actually done something right with my kids.

There is one subject that is guaranteed to push any family to the brink of a breakup: I would rather my husband tell me he's having an affair with a leggy Swede or hear there is another outbreak of head lice at the school than be hit by the announcement at dinnertime that a science fair project is due in the morning.

You send your exhausted ten-year-old to bed at midnight as you finish cutting out the solar system, and your husband is glaring at you from the sofa: "This is the last time you help him—next time he's fails!" But high on glue, you persevere, determined to add a few more planets before morning.

There is surely not a school science fair in the world that is not full of disgruntled and overtired parents sizing one another up, hissing about the sixth grader—and his high-powered engineer father—who wins every year. So the kid invented a hydrofoil that can cross the Atlantic in sixty seconds—everyone knows it was made in Dad's company labs. It's when prizes are given out, though, that the scene gets truly horrifying: glassy-eyed parents sitting on the edge of their plastic seats, knuckles white, hoping against hope that their child's name will be called.

The same goes for homework. If there is a parent out there who can truthfully say he or she hasn't helped with—or more likely done—their kids' homework, please raise your hand. . . . Just as I thought.

6

Mum, it's all your fault!

It was 2001 and I was alone, legging it through the airport in Los Angeles trying desperately not to miss my flight. I had been in some exciting meetings with the Oxygen Network, and was feeling exhilarated, on top of the world. Still, I was looking forward to getting home.

Just as I reached the gate my cellphone rang. It was Max. "Mum, I've failed my math exam and it's all your fault. I have to redo it during the school trip to Boston—which I'm now going to miss!" he wailed.

"That's a bummer," I said, trying to catch my breath. "Don't worry, I'll help you when I'm home."

There was quiet on the other end of the line. "What do you mean? Where are you?"

"I'm in L.A."

"Oh," he mumbled. "I thought you were upstairs."

I had been gone for two days.

I sat on the plane wondering how I was supposed to feel. He was eleven at the time—still a baby in my eyes, but an independent man in his own. Should I be feeling wildly guilty for not being there to comfort him, or laugh, relieved that he was so busy with his own life that it hadn't even registered I was out of town? I'm still not sure.

But I fly a lot, and I do know that I have never seen a businessman sitting in departures sobbing into his phone about missing his daughter's recital. I have never seen a man whispering into his BlackBerry as we are about to take off that his son's homework is under the laundry pile, or that he'll write the note to the teacher when he gets back. Every time I travel, I hear women still running the house-hold via their cellphones as they move from home into work mode.

Travelling puts a huge amount of pressure on working mums—including me—but I have tried over the years to take a page from my male colleagues' book and leave the guilt on the ground at home.

The reality is that life is one big trade-off. You do what you can to make sure your children feel loved and safe. You try to be present when they need you. But if your work is a major part of who you are, and you feel passionate about it, you have to pay attention to that as well. I stayed happy and sane (mostly) through the years because I real-ized early on that even if I wasn't home all the time, even if I was working like mad to build a business, to make my own way in the world, my kids were going to be fine.

Children are incredibly resilient creatures. They *will* get through. And they'll not only survive but admire you for what you have achieved and the fact that you've paid attention to their needs as well as your own.

Life was in full gear for us when the boys were preteens. *The Painted House* was an established hit, and we were moving away from a small cottage-industry production company to a mid-sized organization with all the trials and tribulations that come with growth. We had also begun to explore the idea of translating my TV and video success into other areas (products, books, and so on)—known in business as expanding the brand.

I think sometimes there are real advantages to being short on time, juggling family and work. One of them is that you act quickly and on instinct (I was lucky mine were mostly good). That's exactly how I landed my first publishing deal. I had met a book editor at a gift show in Atlanta where I was selling the how-to videos. She handed me her business card and said that if I ever wrote a book on paint to call her.

Two weeks later, I was in New York City for a network meeting and decided to pay her a visit. Hans was away at the time, and I had to get back to relieve the babysitter by six that evening, so I had half a day to make it happen.

When I arrived, I dialled up the editor. "Hi, my name is Debbie Travis, and I met you a couple of weeks ago. You told me to call?"

She sounded surprised. "Um. Well, the way it works is

you send in a manuscript through your agent," she explained (probably dying to get me off the phone).

"Oh, I don't have a manuscript. I've never written anything. But I'm here!"

"What do you mean exactly—'here'?" she asked.

"I'm in the lobby," I said, trying desperately not to whine.

Bless her heart, she laughed. "Well, you had better come up. I'll give you five minutes."

I could barely breathe as I headed up to the millionth floor in the impressive building that is Random House. Waiting for access to the inner sanctum, I could feel my knees knocking. I felt as if I were stationed outside the headmistress's office back at school. Just then, the door of a neighbouring office flew open and Martha Stewart strode out, exuding all the confidence in the world. Like a small child emulating her mother, I thrust my shoulders back, held my head up high and walked into my first-ever publishing meeting with hope and confidence.

Several weeks later I was offered a book deal, which became the award-winning *Debbie Travis's Painted House,* soon to be followed by seven others.

After I had the publishing deal, though, I was truly swamped, filming most of the year, writing in any spare time and photographing all the homes for the books. Hans was heading up the production company. It only takes one successful show and networks begin to ask you to create other series; we began producing all kinds of lifestyle programs.

Life was hectic and I was tired. The boys, though,

seemed to have boundless energy and a million things on the go—sports and school, guitar lessons, friends and more friends. People would tell me to take a break, but it was easy with stressed-out schedules to pooh-pooh the idea of taking time out to relax and rejuvenate, to be on my own (business trips don't count). I also felt guilty about spending money on myself, walking away from everything when there was so much going on.

But whether you're a multi-tasking working mother or an exhausted stay-at-home mum—or a bit of both—you have to do it. It will take every ounce of your imagination to pull it off—not to mention a few late nights making dinners to freeze for the week ahead—but it's absolutely essential. Just making the decision to leave is often the hardest part.

It finally sank in for me one lovely May afternoon when the boys were eleven and twelve. I had left work early to take them for an ice-cream cone and enjoy the sunshine. I sat outside the café while they were inside, arguing over which flavours to have. I don't know how or why, but sitting there in a sea of plastic white chairs, I began to cry. (Maybe it was the chairs—they'd make anyone depressed.) It was like being in a trance, in a world sealed up by my own misery. Just my luck, one of the kids' teachers sat down beside me. She didn't ask what was wrong, she just said, "It all just gets too much, doesn't it?"

She was right. I was overwhelmed by my life and it had whacked me over the head.

"Take a break," she said. "Just go away for a week."

"Ooh, I couldn't do *that*, I'm—"

She didn't let me finish. "Yes, you can. Just do it."

A few days later, I booked myself into a hiking spa in the northern part of Baja California, Mexico. (Writing this, I can hardly believe I waited until my kids were eleven and twelve to do it, though leaving them for a week when they were younger would have seemed an impossible luxury.) I flew into San Diego, and a bus picked up me and five other guests for the hour drive south to the spa. We were the most miserable, tired-looking bunch I'd ever seen. But as we drove, we started to chat. They all had stories about their lives back home, and all of them were completely exhausted. Every single one of the women felt rotten about "selfishly" taking a week off by herself.

The spa sat in a valley surrounded by mountains, which we climbed every morning. We paused for yoga at sunrise, then spent the day hanging out at the pool, eating healthy food and enjoying every kind of spa treatment you can imagine. It felt like a kids' camp, but for grown-ups. A large group of African-American women who had all met in college and had been visiting the retreat every year for well over two decades were there at the same time. By that point they were in their early fifties, and they were mesmerizing. They roared with laughter and talked incessantly with one another as they hiked or sat around in their bathrobes. One of them told me that the only rule was that they all had to be there the same week every year. The only acceptable excuse for not showing up was a death in the family.

By the time my week was over, all those slouching, bedraggled specimens I'd seen on the bus were changed women. They looked like young girls as they hugged and swapped addresses. One woman shouted to the crowd as we drove away, "This was my best week ever! I didn't hear the words *Muuuum, can I . . . ?* once!" We all cheered.

That one-week break was life changing for me. I have repeated it every year since, in a variety of locations around the world. Several years ago, I hiked across Vietnam with fifty Brits to raise money for colon cancer research. (Treks for charity are an amazing way to have an adventure and do something for a cause—if you think you can't afford a week away, get creative.) We trekked about forty kilometres a day and camped en route. Even though we were all strangers, we talked from early morning—over mugs of piping-hot tea—until we reached the next camp at dusk. There were about thirty-five women and fifteen men (plus ten majestic elephants carrying our bags). On the last day I made a little home movie and asked everyone about the toughest challenge they had faced on the hike. One of the blokes looked straight into the camera and said, "Oh, that's easy—walking with thirty-five women who never shut up!"

When Good Science Fairs Go Bad

The preteen years are a constant tug-of-war. Children are mid-flight in the transformation from needing you at all levels to becoming absorbed in their own lives, trying out independence. They need you and want you one minute, and they don't want to have anything to do with you the next.

Homework is the bridge between their school and home life and ground zero for this tug-of-war. By this point you've learned not to be insulted by single-syllable grunts in response to your daily query, "How was school?" but figuring out how much to help with math and the social studies essay that was due yesterday is brand-new territory.

I don't remember my parents ever–*ever*–helping me with homework, never mind finding a tutor so I kept up in chemistry. My mother's only rule when we got home from school was that we had to change out of our uniforms and there was no television until our homework was finished. My parents certainly never checked to make sure I'd done it (I can't quite imagine what my mum would have made of today's kids who have to have their parents' sign their agenda or initial their homework every day). The way she saw it, the results would show up in our report cards at the end of the school year. We'd have to face the music then. "Deborah could do better" was the constant refrain in my dreaded reports. That's when I'd hear, "You'll be working in the fish market for the rest of your life!" and "Do you want to end up like those women?—no teeth by the time you're thirty!" (She must have figured appealing to my vanity was as good a way as any to get me through school.)

School is different now, of course. Parents are deeply involved in their children's education. It's mostly a good thing, though there are times when it goes too far. The science fair is one of those times. If I were in charge, I'd have it banned. Hans always said that his most dreaded phone call was the one that began, "Can you stop at the store and pick up some bristol board?"

The problem isn't the kids, it's the parents. Each year, one of my boys would be partnered with another child—and his nightmare parent. It would start off friendly enough. "Hey, Mum, I'm working with Gregory on my *How Household Detergent Can Save the World* project." Oh goody, I'd think. Now, Gregory is a fine boy, but his mother is the ultimate Yummy Mummy. I could not envision her kneeling on my kitchen floor, her perfect, designer-jeans-clad bottom in the air, glue and bubbles everywhere. Of course I'm no shrinking violet, either. I have no doubt that any parent who drew me and one of my boys as partners was bemoaning her fate just as loudly. "Oh great, I get the Queen of Craft—how am I supposed to compete with that? *And* she's hideously bossy!"

One time, after spending four consecutive evenings arguing with Mrs. Schwartz about the merits and mechanics of the steam engine (I grew up in the area it was invented, for gawdsake, but wouldn't you know she would pull rank with some dusty old degree in engineering), we displayed our sad-looking exhibit made of two hundred soggy, hand-sprayed toilet-paper rolls and a couple of steaming kettles. We didn't stand a chance—there were projects there that could have been launched into space.

I did achieve victory, however, with Max's Grade 8 science fair project. We were partnered with Clare and her son, Robert, both of whom I liked. We started things off with a meeting around her kitchen table. The kids had some ridiculous idea of a miniature hot-air-balloon demonstration, but we had a far more brilliant plan: a reconstruction of the 1906 San Francisco earthquake. Clare and I were giddy with excitement. We worked night and day, forced to redo all the kids' work, which just wasn't up to par.

Over martinis one evening, we enlisted Clare's husband to invent a control that would make the model shake. Hans joined in as well, rigging the whole contraption up with sound effects from our recording studio. We had ambulance sirens, people screaming and the sound of buildings collapsing.

We entered our masterpiece in the national school science fair—and won! When Max's and Robert's names were called to go and collect their gold medal, my new best friend and I leapt to our feet. Hans had to hold us back. I was so proud. I have won many awards since, but I have to admit that gold medal was one of my lifetime achievements. (Clare and I were asked not to attend the science fair the following year.)

We all want our children to do well and feel good about themselves, so it's hard not to immerse yourself in their schoolwork. But guiding them is one thing, mollycoddling them quite another. It gives them the idea that you don't think they can do it themselves and ultimately devalues their efforts.

I see parents marching into school all the time to complain about such and such a teacher or mark or the number of detentions their boy has served. It is never their child's fault. But we have to let teachers do their job—teaching. After all, they are the ones with the experience; parents are generally new to the job. Ten to one little Johnny is (a) messing around or (b) not up to the task at hand. Sometimes that's a tough pill for parents to swallow.

Of course, there are going to be times when you do need to stand up for your child with teachers and with other kids. Playground bullies must be tackled head-on by the proper authorities (usually the school) and the fire put out as soon as possible. But there is a difference between bullying and teasing, which is just part of life. Comedians will often say that they were teased at school and comedy became their defence. I have an uncle who has a terrible stutter and was teased horribly when he was young. At ten years old, he was enrolled by his mother in theatre school. Today he's one of Britain's most popular speakers, and when we're in England we often go to see him take the stage. He still stutters badly but he laughs at himself and so does the audience. Because of his confidence, though, they laugh *with* him not *at* him.

Josh had a terrible time with teasing in Grade 6. For some strange reason, he went from a popular boy to a boy who got picked on by his friends for several months. I watched from my living room window a number of times as he was shoved into the school hedge on the way home. Tempted to pounce on the other kids and remove their front teeth, I called a friend instead (always a better option). She told me to let him work it out. It was painful, but I took her advice. If we protect them all the time, finish their homework (complete their science projects), defend their every action in the playground, we take away our children's tools for life. They need to learn how to succeed—and how to fail.

I see how true this is in the case of some of my boys' friends now—both male and female. They're in their late teens or early twenties, and they are totally lost. They're struggling with how to deal with real life because all through their childhood they had everything taken care of, every trouble managed by their parents, their lives mapped out for them. Many are popping anti-depressants and Valium to cope with what is a frightening new world.

Raising kids is rather like shaping clay. You work at it and work at it, trying to make sure that they don't have any wobbly bits, that all the scratches are smoothed out, no major dents. Every time something happens, it's a huge thing—the failed exam, the stitches on their chin, the hurt they feel when they get left out of a social scene or dumped by their first girlfriend—and you do what you can to help them get over it. But if you do too much, shelter them entirely from life, fast-forward to their twenties and they'll be unimaginative, needy and helpless. After all, it's the imperfections that give the finished bowl—and the person—character.

It's All in the Preparation

Kids know better than anyone else on the face of the earth how to push their mother's buttons. They are knowing little buggers, and they'll do what they can to raise your blood pressure. The Look is indispensable in stopping them cold, of course, but only part of a larger parenting approach that I think of as the fear factor. It's about respect and firmness, having your children understand that there is a line past which they cannot go with you.

Establishing this fear factor in the preteen years is key. If you don't make that line clear then, you don't have a hope in hell when they're sixteen and towering over you, talking to you as if you are pond scum. I think it's rather like painting and decorating. Your tools for a professional job are preparation and primer. You can't cut corners—skip the sanding and filling, or skimp on primer—because it's guaranteed (and I know this stuff) that within a couple of months the old stains and cracks will poke through and the paint will start to peel. It's the same with preteens. Preparation is key. Establish the rules, the punishments and the guidelines with a firmness that may seem harsh, and your life will be a bit—just a bit—easier when the teenage years arrive.

My mother set the tone in our house with her temper. We were never beaten (smacked and swiped on the back of the head occasionally); instead, she used her tongue as her weapon. Sometimes words hurt even more than a spanking, and I have tried very hard with my own children not to begin a sentence with "you"—"*You* are destructive" or "*You've* ruined our day." It just gets too personal when you focus on them as individuals rather than on their snot-nosed behaviour.

My husband, on the other hand, was regularly given a beating—no, not by me, by his mother with *her* weapon of choice, a wooden cooking spoon. As a result, he's never laid a finger on our kids. It's easy to be righteous about this. No one is going to be flawless. We all do things we regret in the heat of our busy, complicated lives. I lost it once having a large group picture taken with my kids and all their little cousins. Josh was small at the time, and it was impossible to get him to stay still. I finally manhandled him in front of me, holding him in a fierce grip, smile plastered on my face for the photo. In the process, I accidentally scratched the front of his tender young chest. He still has a tiny scar there (which he likes to tease me about every so often). I hate myself every time I see it.

Being firm can be incredibly hard. (And if you think it's hard for couples, imagine the pressure on the single parent who must play both good cop and bad cop in these scenarios—they never get a break.) We all devise ways to make our lives easier, whether it's putting on the TV and letting the kids veg out or buying them stuff to keep them quiet or "forgetting" to follow through on a threat because it turned out to be inconvenient (for you). It's easy to come up with screaming punishments like "That's it! You're not coming on vacation with us!" But when both of you know you're not going to follow through, they realize that they can walk all over you.

Punishments can be extremely inventive. I had a cousin who was just plain boring—or that's how I felt when we were both eleven. He was coming over for a visit, so I climbed into a neighbour's field and shovelled up a bucket full of cow poo. When he arrived, I was up on the garage roof, the manure rolled into steaming, smelly cannonballs. I spent a happy half-hour lobbing him with balls of dung. (I was very immature for my age.) Needless to say, I was in major trouble and my mother told Jonathan he could choose my punishment.

"I would like Debbie to come trainspotting with me for the rest of the afternoon," he said, gloating, I'm sure, because he knew I would rather have washed down the driveway (which my mother made me do anyway).

By the end of that sunny afternoon lying on our stomachs at the edge of the railway line, we'd become firm friends. He is still there for me today (though I do watch my back in case he decides to get his revenge!).

Hans and I tended to stick with punishments that, we thought, fitted the crime (and there were many). After school one day I smelled something burning in the house and ran around like a large bloodhound until I realized it was coming from Josh's room. I sprinted up the stairs and flung open the door. There he was, sitting at his desk looking guilty, his school tie a melted nylon mass down the front of him. He'd been studying and had become bored, so he set his school tie on fire. Why? Just to see if it would burn. I was furious and despite pleading from both him and the headmaster, I made him wear the nasty half-burnt flap of fabric the rest of the year. (Whatever else it achieved, it certainly quelled any thoughts he might have had about becoming a serial arsonist.)

But the bad behaviour of preteens has nothing on what is to come once they hit thirteen. There's still an innocence about younger kids, which makes even their disobedience sort of funny. Of course, that's changing somewhat as children (especially girls) are growing up much faster. My nieces can swing within the space of a second from sweet little girls playing with Barbies to miniature teens singing along to Hannah Montana with all the hip-thrusting attitude and language of much older kids.

To me, it is important that early on you instill in your children a sense of the consequences of their actions and respect for the people around them. It's not easy. We nearly threw in the towel on a spring break ski trip to Whistler, B.C. After an endless flight, then car trip, we arrived at a four-star hotel at the bottom of the famous mountain. The boys immediately disappeared to explore while we unpacked and sneaked in a midday snooze. Thinking they were mature enough to wander around the hotel on their own, we left them to it. An hour later, the manager was on the phone asking us to please come and remove our children from the lobby.

Apparently they had ganged up with some British boys and had started a snowball fight across the heated outdoor pool, hitting countless older people smack in the face. They had been reprimanded several times, then banned altogether. And if that wasn't bad enough, they'd then headed for the men's locker room, where they covered all the mirrors with shaving cream and scrawled rude words into the mess. Madly funny when you're eleven years old—not so much for the hotel and a seething, overtired father. When they returned to our room, Hans dragging them by the scruff of the neck, he picked up the phone and dialled the airline. They were going to go home alone while we stayed and enjoyed our holiday. (You've got to love families—we'd been on vacation for no more than a couple of hours!) I knew Hans was faking, but the boys sobbed while they packed their bags.

Suddenly there was a knock at the door. A student in charge of the men's locker room was standing there when we opened up (secretly arranged by Super Mum from the cellphone in the bathroom). "It wasn't that bad, sir," he tried to say.

But Hans would have none of it. He was truly angry, until the kid (at my secret suggestion), offered a punishment we couldn't refuse. The boys would be allowed to ski in the morning, but in the afternoon they would work his area. It was ideal. I'd see them walk by on the deck carrying hors d'oeuvres, or folding towels. Of course, for them, it was the best vacation ever, because they got to meet all the older kids who worked there. But they also learned about Hans's wrath and just how far we were willing to go. The fear factor sank in. Victory to Mum and Dad!

Television and computer games are another key battleground in these years. Negotiating the terms—how much, what kinds of game and programs—can require an advanced law degree on a parent's part. "I'll give you one hour of video games for one hour of reading."

"One and a half!" they'll counter. "And I'll throw in a tutorial on the TV remote!"

Report card time is an excellent moment to establish your own negotiating power in this department. Standing in the kitchen one year, Hans read the report cards out loud to all of us. The boys tried to appear calm while their little minds whirled with every excuse in the book: "The whole class did terribly! Really! Mrs. Jones said 27 per cent is good, considering."

But Hans was fed up. He disappeared into our basement and reappeared carrying our one and only television. "This is going to the office until your next report cards come in," he said. "And they'd better improve!" It took a year until he finally brought the TV back. (God, I was miserable!)

I worry about all the technology our children are

growing up with, because they're missing out on entire chunks of their childhood while they're plugged into a video game. And it's not just kids. I see mothers dropping off their children at the school across the street, driving these oversized SUVs that could probably cross a desert, talking on their cellphones, tapping away on their BlackBerrys—all while applying lipstick. Right up until they graduated, I would watch Max and Josh until they were inside the front door of the school because I thought these multi-taskers would plow right into them.

I have to admit that I, too, am attached to a "CrackBerry"—as if it's a third limb poking through my right hand. I am ashamed to say that if they had been around when my kids were younger, I would have found it hard not to peek at that tantalizing screen. I admire my neighbour Helen, the doctor with two young kids. She doesn't own a cellphone or an iPod. She rarely even answers her home phone—I have to throw stones at her window to get her attention. "My time with the kids is now. I'm not sharing it nattering on the phone," she says. "All I need is my pager for medical emergencies—no, you can't have the number."

Helen is absolutely right. All these devices are supposed to make us more connected, but there's nothing more *dis*connected than to have your child on the computer and you on your cell, never really speaking to each other. It's also hard to break this bad habit: before you know it, you're the mother of the bride texting someone while you're waiting for your daughter's grand entrance at the front of the church (don't laugh—I've seen it).

It would be a shame to miss out on this part of your kids' life. They have a cleverness and charm that is wickedly fun—even when they're being naughty. It was around this time that Hans and I had a dinner party with a bunch of friends—the boys gathered on the stairs, listening carefully to our conversation as they loved to do when we entertained—and someone asked me about the key to success. We'd been into the wine by then and I was glad to hold forth.

"Surround yourself with people who are more talented than you," I announced. "They will make your work look so much better." (It's an attitude I've had since the beginning and believe to this day. Most people are afraid of being outshone, but for me it's been a guiding principle.)

A week or so later, we were summoned to the school. Josh had used the money from his allowance and paid a classmate to do his homework. Hans and I took him aside that night and told him sternly that cheating is the worst thing you can do.

"But I didn't cheat," he said.

"Of course you did—you paid someone else to do your work."

"But you said, 'Hire the best.' So I hired Charles Wong. He's the best. He even goes to school on weekends."

I gave Josh my most piercing version of the Look—though, privately, Hans and I laughed our heads off.

The transformation from child to teenager seems to happen overnight. Your gorgeous little lad kisses you on the cheek with "Love you, Mummy! I'm going up to bed now." You ruffle his shiny thick hair and smile at your angel. Eight hours later you greet him at breakfast.

"What can I get you to eat, sweetheart?"

"Whatever," he mumbles from underneath his baseball cap, unwashed hair poking through. And what are those red things all over his face? His nose seems to have grown and left his face behind. His arms hang, apelike, around his knees. And his jeans, instead of fitting around his waist, are under his ass, grotty underwear sticking a foot out the top.

"What about a boiled egg?" you ask shakily, uncertain if it is, indeed, your child.

"Stop picking on me!" he yells, and storms from the room, slamming the door behind him.

You stand there, bewildered, horrified. But get used to it—because it's going to be like this for the next few years. Of course, this is just the boys. My heart aches for the parents of girls. Welcome to living with teenagers.

7

Leave it alone
or you'll go blind!

So you think you're starting to get the hang of this parenting thing. Finally, after years of being woken up before any farm animal, you're the one dragging them out of bed every morning (revenge, sweet revenge). They're old enough to stay on their own, so you no longer need to be employing military strategy (coordinating babysitters, play dates, extracurriculars) just to get to a spinning class or a movie. You're hitting your stride in your career. You think you might just be reclaiming a bit of that singleton freedom. But don't get too comfortable!

I received one of the most important calls of my career when I was out with the boys buying jeans. Max and Josh had just entered their teens, and it was the day before we were to leave for a working vacation in Italy. Both kids were in the changing rooms at Urban Outfitters when my cell rang. It was someone from my office.

"Oprah Winfrey just called." The entire store seemed to freeze. "They want you next week."

I couldn't contain my excitement. "Oprah wants me!" I shouted. The news started trickling through the store. Everyone was watching. Everyone, that is, except for my children, who were thumping each other behind a grubby curtain, completely oblivious. "You can't buy the same ones as me! You always copy me!"

Shoppers and staff gathered around. The manager even turned down the pounding music so I could call Oprah's producer. Everyone in the store stood waiting with bated breath.

"We're really looking forward to having you, Debbie—we are such fans of your work here," she said. "How's next Wednesday?"

My heart sank, and panic set in. "Yes, well, I have a wee problem. I'm off to Italy tomorrow for spring break and to film some segments of *The Painted House,* but I'll absolutely sort it out."

I looked over at my beloved children, evil thoughts of abandonment and having them adopted—that afternoon—running through my head. "I'll call you straight back. It's *so* no big deal."

I immediately phoned my publisher in New York City. "Ohmigod!" she said. "This is fantastic for book sales! Drop everything. We'll fly you there. We'll come with you!"

"But we're leaving on vacation tomorrow," I cried.

"Don't go!"

I could hear the boys still arguing, the flimsy wall attached to the change rooms shaking because the inevitable shoving had begun. *I'm just going to leave them here,* I thought. *No one will ever know.*

I called an executive at my network. "Drop everything," he said. "Tell them you don't have kids."

Finally, I reached Hans, who had gone on ahead to Italy—Mr. Doom and Gloom, Mr. Spoil Everything. "That's great," he said. "But there is not a chance you are ruining our shoot and the kids' holiday. You have to come here tomorrow."

"I could put them on a plane!" I pleaded.

"I am *not* taking care of those boys and doing the filming on my own. If Oprah wants you, she'll want you in six months," he said.

"You mean I can't go?"

The whole store was following my conversation, going ooooh and aaaah like fans at a sporting match. I could hear people at the back of the shop who didn't have a good vantage point asking, "What did he say?"

One woman shouted, "He's right! If they want you . . ."

They'll never want me again! I thought, my desperation growing.

Finally, the kids emerged from the change room and I told them what had happened.

"Cool," they mumbled. "You should go, Mum."

But I knew deep down that Hans was right. I called Oprah's producer back. "I'm so sorry, but it's spring break and we're shooting in Italy, and I just can't get away."

"It's fine. Don't worry. We'll get someone else."

"Don't get someone else!"

"No, no, it's fine," she said and put down the phone.

I stood there, my head hanging. The girl behind the cash burst into tears. "I *so* feel for you! I'll take your kids," she offered.

"You don't want them!"

I practically pushed the boys outside and into the car. There was a ticket on the windshield, which I ripped up and dropped at the feet of the ticket man like a petulant toddler.

The kids didn't say a word the entire way home. They could see I was in a zone. *Don't even look at her. Don't say one word about her forgetting to buy the jeans.*

Hans was right, of course. A few months later, Oprah's people called me back to invite me on the show again. And not just as part of a segment with lots of designers; I was to sit next to her and talk about what I do, just have fun. Which is exactly what we did.

Being on *Oprah* was the thrill of a lifetime. It opened many doors and sold lots of books. Even the kids got a huge kick out of it, because all their teachers were addicted to her show. Over the next few years, I was lucky enough to repeat the experience several times.

Life was brimming over. We'd completed two hundred episodes of *The Painted House,* five of my eight books had been published by Random House, and we'd just embarked on my new television adventure, *Facelift.* I'd also begun a syndicated newspaper column answering readers' design questions, which would appear in seventy newspapers across North America.

I was so busy, flying back and forth to L.A. and New York, that it was easy to get muddled. One morning after I'd returned from California, I woke up with a start and dragged Max (Josh was on a trip) out of bed to go to school.

I was at the front door in my PJs waiting for him to come downstairs. He rarely ate breakfast, just slid into his clothes and dragged himself across the road. As I stood there, I thought our street seemed eerily quiet. A lonely jogger slumped by. The milkman—we still have one—rattled up the hill. Max slipped out the door, and as I waved goodbye, it hit me. I ran to look at the clock in the kitchen. It was not eight but five in the morning. I was still on L.A. time. I raced to the front door. "Max! Come back! It's too early for school," I yelled down the street.

Max turned around and looked at me as if I were a green-skinned alien standing stark naked on his front step. There is nothing more heinous to a teenager than being robbed of three hours' sleep.

"We could put on a movie? You know, bond?" I offered.

Max just looked at me, eyebrows arched in disdain. "You know what? You're not like other mothers," he said. "You're just odd."

However fabulous and exciting your life gets, kids will always bring you back down to earth. You just can't have an ego when there are children around—always ready to burst your bubble. On television, I would be talking to hundreds of thousands of captivated people in the comfort of their own living rooms, but at home I was just Mum, cooking and cleaning up for two grouchy teenage boys.

I would be reminded of this again on the night I received two major awards in front of all my television peers. It was truly wonderful just to be nominated, and I was dressed to kill for the fancy gala. When I was named Host of the Year for *The Painted House*, our table, packed with our tight-knit team, went nuts. And before they'd entirely finished cheering, I was called up again for *Facelift*. We went crazy! Filled with the thrill of the moment, I wanted to call home and tell the boys.

I'd actually left earlier that day in something of a huff. I'd shown my fancy dress to Hans. "Gee, that looks comfy," he'd said. I stormed off. *Comfy?* Sex bomb was more like it!

I'd gone to ask Max for a second opinion. He's always been the most stylish of my bunch. He told me I looked beautiful, and as I turned to go out the door, my flagging self-esteem buoyed by his nod, he said, "Even if your bum wobbles when you walk."

Still, I wanted the boys to share our brilliant achievement, so I crawled under the table, cellphone pressed against my ear to hear over the yelling and clapping. Max answered.

"Uh-huh?"

"You'll never guess what happened: I won Host of the Year—not once but twice!"

"Nice, Mum," he said. "Can I call you back—I'm on the other line." (Note to self: cancel all future college fees.)

Testosterone Tornado

Family dynamics are constantly in flux. It's something I have witnessed it in my own home, especially in the teen years, but it really hit me over the head when we began to create *Facelift*, one of the first-ever reality television shows about renovation.

Having spent nearly seven years watching the families on *The Painted House*, and earlier when I was painting people's homes, I knew it would be riveting television if we could capture the highs and lows of renovating, and the family drama that comes into play. Throw in a time limit and forty tradespeople trying to do their job in a confined space, and you can get every kind of emotion—from tears of anger to shouts of joy—all squeezed into an hour-long program.

I'd actually had the idea for the show rattling around in my head for years because of something that happened when I was a teenager. I was not especially pleasant at that age—in fact, I was downright miserable. My mother's new husband, John Travis, was a good, kind man, but totally different from my father, and at first I resented him taking my dad's place in our home.

I even refused to take his name at first. I had previously been known as Debbie Short (not much fun when you're the tallest girl in the class!), and though Travis was an improvement, I was against being formally adopted, stamped forever with a new name.

My sisters were younger and sweeter and readily accepted him. "Goodnight, Daddy," they would say at bedtime, while I sullenly shook his hand. For my brother, Will, who was only a toddler when our mother remarried, John became the only father he knew. Looking back, I know John adored my mother, and they had a good life together. I also grew to love him, but for those first few years I made the sulk into an art form.

When I was at my very worst—sometime around fourteen or fifteen—my mother and stepfather decided to take us all on a family holiday. With my early punk hairdo, sloppy clothes and bad attitude, I loathed the thought of hanging with my family, and I'm sure, deep down, the feeling was mutual. So my mother allowed me to stay at home on the one condition that my grandmother move in while they were gone. (Luckily, I preferred her company to theirs anyway.)

As soon as the family had turned the corner at the end of our street, the two of us hatched a plan to surprise them on their return. We would make over my mother's hallway!

As a girl I had often experimented with moving furniture around—even painting the walls—but had never been allowed to venture outside my own bedroom. This was to be a first. We went to the shop and bought home numerous rolls of cheap flowery wallpaper. By the time we'd done two lengths, we knew we were in way too deep, but there was no going back. We kept cutting the strips of paper

short, causing large gaps at the bottom or top of the wall—
often both. And we couldn't figure out how to match the
pattern, so the rolls either overlapped with long linear
bumps, or there were huge spaces. And that was just the
hallway! By the time we tackled the stairs, it was truly dia-
bolical. Glue was everywhere, including all over Granny,
the carpet and the furniture. Halfway up, we gave up.

When my family returned, Granny was sent packing
back to Liverpool on the bus—"What were you thinking,
Mother??" my mum shouted. "And you!" she screamed at
me. "Get a scraper and get to work."

That incident became the premise of *Facelift*. The idea
was that while one member of a family went away for a
few days, the rest orchestrated a surprise makeover (hopefully with better results than Granny and I had). The show
was an instant hit and became a family favourite around
the world. We were soon receiving nine hundred emails a
day from people pleading to have their home made over
on the show. (Many of the requests were from women pre-
tending to be their husbands. "Oh, she works so hard, and
she's such a great mum," they'd lie. "You have to give her
a new kitchen!")

To me, compelling television happens when viewers
can relate to the program. *Facelift* really hit a nerve
because we all have families and we'd all love a free home
makeover—the twist, and the thing that made it such a big
hit, was the surprise factor. Our motto was, Be careful
what you wish for!

Even our team didn't know what was going to happen. We spent weeks prepping for the show, sneaking into the house to take photographs to work from. (If the person found out, the story would have to be cancelled—to everyone's dismay.) We hid in bushes, on roofs and in ditches to capture them on tape leaving the house. We were lucky enough to find a guy who had worked on the infamous *Candid Camera* to help us hide tiny cameras in plants, among piles of towels, even once inside a radio. All this to find out what exactly they envisioned as their dream space. We captured amazing stuff (most of it not appropriate for family viewing).

During the renovation, we worked like madmen to complete the job in a few days. The carpenters and painters often slept on the floor of the house, since there wasn't enough time to return to the hotel. The pressure of the short timeframe—usually four days—caused a huge amount of stress, but it also made for fantastic television. We'd arrive with these gigantic trucks, take over the house and equipment would be piled in every spare room. We just followed the puck. If neighbours dropped by or the nosy mother-in-law came in to meddle, we'd film them, too. The fretters and the fussers, the micromanagers, the criers—we captured it all.

It was a privilege to spend so much time with these families, each of whom we came to know really well. I was fascinated to see that in all the shows, the mother who went away (it was often a woman) would call her family at least ten times a day for the first two days. She would have a constant list of questions. Has the dog been fed? Is the homework finished? How was soccer? It was endless. But after that, she'd find her own groove, relax a bit, and I would see how Dad and the kids also carried on with their lives. Even though most of the mums believed they were the only thing keeping the house together, the family actually coped pretty well in her absence—a lesson for me in understanding my own brood.

By the time we were creating *Facelift,* Hans had moved from behind the camera to behind a desk at the office (he says he quit directing; I say I fired him!). We also roped in the boys whenever we could. They needed pocket money, and I thought they should have to work for it, so during school breaks we'd find them a job on set. We'd use them as navvies, hauling gear around, setting up equipment. They loved to hang out with the crew, and whenever possible would stay over, pitching a tent and spending the night swapping stories with the guys.

Watching them on set, I saw clearly that our boys had really grown up. It was fascinating—bordering on terrifying—to witness. All of a sudden their voices had gone from girly to manly with only a short squeaky bit inbetween. And with all the single-syllable mumbling, we could hardly understand a word they said. (A schoolteacher of this age group is a brave person indeed. "Move your lips, pleeease!" they must have to say a million times a day.)

The stiffy became a constant fixture in our house in the

morning. (Wake them up and you are saluted, watch them leave the bathroom and you could hang a towel on it!) And they never seem to take their hand out of their pants. They will stand chatting with anyone—their grandfather, math teacher or best buddy—hand nestled safely on their privates. "I'm a style guru!" I'd tell them. "Would you please take your hand out of your crotch in public?"

For parents, this change can be traumatic, and today many schools actually have a parent evening to warn people what to expect. Our all-boys' school held a special night to discuss the Testosterone Tornado. The teachers stood at the front of the auditorium looking smug, laughing at our shell-shocked faces. They'd seen it all before.

Teenagers live in a bubble in which only their own species is welcome. The rest of us are morons. Their room becomes their nest—sometimes for weeks at a time. You begin to realize that's where the *Victoria's Secret* catalogues that used to pile up in the front hall have mysteriously disappeared to, and that knocking before you enter their bedroom is not just about *their* privacy, it's to protect you from something no mother should have to see.

They will honour you occasionally by joining the family at mealtimes. Unfortunately, they can eat enough to feed a small nation in one sitting. I once witnessed one of my boys' friends cut an unsliced loaf of bread down the middle and place a joint of beef that would feed a family of ten between the slabs. "Oh hi, Ms. T," he said, looking up. "Just helping myself to a snack. Hope you don't mind."

"No worries, Ivan, that was just our weekend roast," I offered blithely.

It was then that my Costco days came to an end. I love a megastore as much as the next mum, but each time I drove home, I would start to get the sweats five minutes from our house, then heart palpitations. I'd turn the car engine off as I came down the hill, try to roll silently into the driveway. Still, the boys would be waiting, ready to pounce. Though they are still not clear on the function of the dishwasher, have no clue about how to work the washing machine, think dish soap is for cleaning bikes, they are nonetheless highly skilled in detecting a trunkful of groceries. And it wasn't just my own children. The whole neighbourhood would be there: skinny little girls who never ate except at our house, boys who could inhale an entire box of cookies before the trunk was closed.

"Hey! Can we help unload?" they'd drool. I'd try to beat them off, but it was always too late. Juice boxes—forget it— they wouldn't even get in the house. A trail of cookie, bread and chip crumbs littered the hall. I would arrive at my long, Tuscan-style kitchen table—the dumping ground for everything—and all that would be left was the house-hold cleaners and a supersized bag of broccoli.

My friend Danielle has four teenage boys. They are all football players, and each one is built like a large fridge. Over coffee one day, she let me in on her secret for not going broke due to astronomical food bills. She unbuttoned the top of her shirt to show me a key hanging around her neck.

"So?" I shrugged.

"I put a padlock on the fridge and carry the key with me at all times," she explained. "If they want to eat, they have to wait for me—or go elsewhere."

Which, of course, is why her giants are always hanging around my house!

It was in those years, as our growing boys began to tower over us, that Hans came into his own as a parent. They were suddenly more comfortable with him and gave him a new sort of respect. I had always been the disciplinarian—a constant nag, really. Now I needed a stepladder to battle them eye to eye. Hans began to take over that role, while I became the softie they could cuddle up to because Dad was so mean (I recommend this—it's so much more pleasant to be the good cop).

Hans also seemed to know just what to do about the influx of testosterone that was making our very walls shudder. One night, the two of us were sitting in our tiny little den. It's the coziest room with two fat club chairs and a real wood-burning fireplace. We were relaxing, sipping wine and chatting—a rare moment. Josh blasted down the stairs waving a catalogue in his hand. "*Victoria's Secret* isn't doing it for me anymore," he moaned, apparently in agony.

I was in shock, but my sensitive hubby leapt to attention. "Let's go," he said.

"You're going to go blind!" I shouted as they slammed the door and squealed out the driveway.

I called Josh an hour later to see where they'd gone. He

was sitting in the car outside a magazine shop. His father was inside working his way through "the top shelf," and had been for forty-five minutes.

When they arrived home, Josh headed straight back to his room carrying a plastic bag packed with magazines. "That's disgusting!" I called after him.

But deep down I was really quite proud that he could be so open with us. I never would have dared to talk about sex or anything related to it with my parents. Of course, maturity on these matters was not always evident. We never had the sex talk, despite the advice of parenting books, because my boys just screamed with laughter every time I approached the subject of safe sex. So instead, *I* attended helpful lectures at the school with titles like "The Parent and the Popular Penis" and "From the Clap to the Condom"—all the while squished on a school bench between a Yummy Mummy and some dodgy dad who pressed his thigh unnecessarily into mine. Still, I did pick up one tip that I thought sounded smart: don't say a word to your kids but stock a drawer with condoms, knowing they'll find them and use them if required, without having to be embarrassed.

I didn't think my boys *required* them quite yet, but, I figured, I'd be a cool, modern mum and do as the experts suggested. I had never bought a condom in my life, but I bravely filled a shopping basket with every shape and size. There I was in my local pharmacy, basket brimming with enough prophylactics to protect the entire student population of Fort Lauderdale at spring break, and who do I bump into but the dodgy dad. When he saw what I was carrying, he smiled the creepiest smirk—I think he thought I was about to invite him home for a jolly good afternoon. Instead, I rushed back to the safety of my bathroom and stocked every drawer, thinking what a clever, thoughtful mum I was.

The following weekend I was parking outside our house and noticed my small front garden littered with what resembled deflated balloons. Suspicious, I moved in to inspect. Of course it was the condoms.

Just then, my neighbour appeared out of nowhere. He was absolutely sopping wet.

"Mrs. Travis? Could you give me a ballpark timeframe about when your kids will be leaving home?" he said.

"Why? What happened?" I asked, my heart sinking.

"Well, about fifteen minutes ago, this was a war zone. There were a bunch of delinquents in your bedroom window lobbing water balloons at another bunch dashing around your front lawn. As you can see," he said, kicking a pale pink slither of wet latex off the end of his foot. "Unfortunately, I got caught in the crossfire."

When Bad Things Happen

My kids made many solid friendships in those early teen years. There is an intensity to relationships at that age and an ease kids have with one another—their friends even begin to replace their family in some ways. They talk on the phone for hours and hours and can be fiercely loyal and protective. I found it a joy to watch these relationships develop—and heartbreaking when things went wrong.

When Max was in Grade 9, he had a small posse of mates, all in the same class. One of the boys was Addy, a tall, handsome Hindu boy who seemed to have missed the awkward stage many of his age group were stuck in.

Max and Addy were study buddies, and one warm June evening before their final French exam, they were working together over the phone, Addy at his house, Max at ours. I knew Max was multi-tasking—playing guitar, chatting on both his cell and the home phone, a game up on the screen, all while supposedly studying for his final. I barged in and told him he would have to stop—no more chatting, just studying. Alone. Addy told Max he was going to a barbecue held at his old school, and was going to blow off some steam and play basketball in the gym there.

The next day, I was shooting *Facelift* and got a call on set. It was Max. He was in shock. Addy was dead. The court where he'd gone to shoot hoops was new, and had not been built properly or tested. While he was playing, a wall of cement blocks collapsed on him. He died in hospital that night. He was fifteen years old.

The school brought in experts to talk to the kids. But the boys didn't want to talk, they wanted to honour their friend—and they wanted to do it right away. Max and his classmates decided planting a tree on the school grounds would be a fitting tribute.

They approached the headmaster with their idea, but he told them no, not yet. The kids were furious. These gawky young boys seemed to grow into young men before my eyes as they tackled the tragic situation head-on.

They figured they could plant their tree somewhere else right away, so a small mob marched down to our town hall near the school to inquire. The elderly lady sitting at the desk had probably seen it all over the years (hysterical home-owners fighting over permits for their reno, neighbours squabbling over backyard parties), but I'm pretty certain she had never witnessed twenty determined kids who demanded a tiny section of park to plant a tree—immediately.

Something in their haunted teenage faces must have hit a chord, because the lady at the town hall agreed. They just had to get a tree. Three of the boys leapt into my brand-new convertible, and the rest dashed off to find buckets and spades. An hour later, we had a young maple hanging out the back of my car, ready to go in the ground. That's were I left them to do their own thing.

I watched from my front lawn as the group of boys, now forty-strong, followed the elderly lady up the road to the park, some of them carrying tools, others the beautiful red maple tree. With no teachers or parents around, the boys dug the hole and planted the tree in their friend's name. Later that afternoon, they set off on their bikes to a sign maker and had a plaque made.

I was so proud of Max and his friends for what they did, for taking charge and figuring out a way to deal with their grief on their own terms. They were impatient and unwilling to go through the usual channels, but that's the way it is with teenagers. They were full of rage and sadness, and planting a tree seemed to me like a pretty great way to channel that energy. I still drive past that red maple nearly every day. It's been several years now, and it is thriving. Addy's family has visited. Each time I see it, it reminds me of the extraordinary strength and compassion of children.

All a parent dreams about for their kids is that they make it to adulthood in one piece with even the hope of future happiness. But you know that horrible, unexpected, unfair things can happen, and as they get older each stage seems more frightening than the next. You just hope and hope and hope, cross your fingers that your child will be okay.

Sometimes, of course, it's not disaster you worry about so much as simply getting through to them. There have been countless studies about kids in this age group, including research that shows about 10 per cent of young people become clinically depressed during their teens (a figure that researchers think is probably the same as it's ever been, though now kids have more opportunities to talk about it).

As they pull away from you and the rest of their family, it can be tempting as a parent to pull away yourself, but this is the time when we must make a conscious effort to be around—even if they don't particularly want to be near us. Just the knowledge that their parents are holding down the family fort, that rules are in place, and you are home when they return at night is imperative. Fighting with your teenagers is normal, and if you look at the big picture, it doesn't actually last that long.

Teens often need space just to sort through their feelings on their own terms. I was twelve when my father died, and those years following his death are still crystal clear to me. Every morning, I would walk down the stairs mumbling a wish that he would be sitting at the kitchen table. I started off every day with a heavy heart.

I also spent hours by myself searching for his grave. My siblings and I weren't allowed to attend his funeral, since it was thought to be too upsetting. But this was wrong. I didn't even know where he was buried—and I was damned if I was going to ask. I began by walking through grave-yards in the surrounding villages. (Sounds weirdly mor-bid, but I had no one I could talk to.) I found him one day when I was fourteen and waiting for the bus to take me into town to meet my friends. I was sitting on the stone wall surrounding the graveyard in an adjacent vil-lage. I was bored (there is nothing worse than being dependent on the country bus), and I swung my legs over the cemetery side of the wall. When I looked down, right beside my boot was a plaque, no bigger than a standard sheet of office paper, with my father's name on it.

I leapt down and looked more closely. He'd been cre-mated. I felt surprisingly happy with my discovery, and also comforted that he had been there all along as I sat on that wall, in that same spot, at that same bus stop for two years.

Of course it would have been easier if I'd just asked my mother about it, but teenagers do not do things the easy way. They need to find their way to adulthood, create their own rites of passage. It can be painful and slow, but they get there in their own time.

The Evil Pleasure of Embarrassing Your Teenager

The years between thirteen and fifteen are the hanging-out years. Teenagers at that age want to be as far away as possible from their parents (except, of course, when they need money or food), but they're too young for bars and clubs and other adult places. It's always a challenge to find a spot to go, and I'm convinced that's why kids this age get into trouble.

When I was growing up, we had nowhere to hang out in the village, so we ended up in fields with the boys perfecting our smoking skills and swigging stolen cooking sherry. My own children spent endless evenings hanging out in our local park. When school was out I insisted on a curfew of midnight, which they would constantly ignore. I could never sleep until everyone was home—so annoying when you have to be up early. And I also had the added challenge of having to look bright-eyed and gorgeous on a TV set the following morning.

I was fed up with them always being late, so one night when they had stayed out twenty minutes past their curfew,

I marched down to collect them. I stood in the middle of the park shouting, "Max! Josh!" wearing nothing but my PJs and rollers (which I added for extra effect). They never did it again. It's a technique I learned from my stepfather, who would mortify me at the same age by barging onto the dance floor of the youth club with his pyjamas sticking out the bottom of his trousers.

Soon the boys found a new place to hang out: the coffee shop down the road. Naturally, such establishments aren't exactly thrilled to have hordes of teens sitting there for hours with empty pockets, so the kids found a way to make themselves more welcome. I figured out what they were doing one day when I was rummaging in the cigar box Josh had in his room filled with money (mostly gifts from grandparents). I was just borrowing a couple of dollars (you know how you do!) when I noticed it was virtually empty (and it wasn't me). Turns out that he'd been buying rounds of $4 superdeluxe caramel, double-moccaccino designer coffees for all his friends, as if he were some big shot in a bar buying bottles of champagne. I was so shocked that I dragged him down to the café and balled out the sullen barista for allowing kids to blow their money like that. It wasn't the barista's fault, of course, but Josh was sufficiently mortified that he kept his money tucked away after that.

Embarrassment is a key tool in raising teens. They are extremely thin-skinned, and even the threat of being embarrassed (it doesn't take much) is often enough to keep them in line. In fact, just the mention of parental nudity will send them into agonies of shame. When we visited my best friend's place in Spain when the kids were young, I would often go topless—like every other woman on these European beaches. But when we planned a trip after they hit puberty, the boys made me promise I wouldn't even dream of stripping off. (As if I would, but more for my own vanity—by then I wouldn't have wanted to horrify my fellow sunbathers.)

When the boys were fourteen and fifteen, Hans and I were bumped to first class on our way to Malaga. We left them in economy and enjoyed the fruits of our labour: better food and free drinks. We were really starting to get into it when Max elbowed his way through the dividing curtain. "It's not fair!" he said. "We're stuck in the back and you guys get these comfy seats."

We ignored him as we sipped our champagne, and he skulked back to his brother. But it wasn't long before Josh came forward himself. He'd begun his own fairness campaign, weeks earlier, trying to get us to agree to have their curfew extended once we got to Spain. We were planning to stay at a holiday villa owned by friends who had kids slightly older than our pair. They'd been given permission to go to clubs and stay out late. "It's not *fair* they get to hang out until 2 a.m., and we have to be home by midnight," Josh complained. "It's just not *fair*." This mantra had been repeated incessantly for weeks as the holiday approached.

I was beginning to get irritated with them for disturbing our first-class reverie, and I began to hatch a plan. Soon the two of them arrived together.

"You're not going to go topless, are you, Mum?" asked Max.

"I know you said twelve but the others can stay out until two. How about 1 a.m.?" Josh offered, as if we were in negotiations.

I was finally fed up. "I've said midnight, and if you come in one minute after, I guarantee you will find me playing volleyball stark naked on the beach with your father in the morning."

That was the last we saw of them on the flight.

I'm still giggling about that one. The glee of getting one up on a teenager is not to be underestimated. There are moments, however, when even I know I've gone a teensy bit too far. I'm not sure if Josh will ever forgive me for the night I received the Crystal Award for Creative Excellence given out by the organization Women in Film and Television.

I was really proud when I heard about the award; I was especially thrilled because I've made it a priority to create opportunities for young women who have that same love of the industry that I do. All my peers were going to be there, and I asked the boys if they'd like to come too. I might as well have asked them to eat gum off the bottom of my shoe. "You mean, two weeks from tomorrow? What? Uh, I'm busy."

But when I mentioned that Kim Cattrell, Samantha the sex bomb from *Sex and the City,* was also going to be honoured that night, Josh revised his plans. "I just think she's a really great actress," he told me, blushing.

That night, we had a large table and invited many of the people who'd supported me over the years. Josh was quite self-conscious at the time, but he seemed to hold up well. Kim Cattrell spoke first and gave a very funny scripted talk all about sex and the TV industry. She had the crowd in the palm of her hand.

The more she went on, the more I worried about following her on the stage. I'd written quite a formal speech, thanking the people who'd helped me along the way, but I left it on the table and just spoke from the heart. I talked about how TV is not a nine-to-five job, how women who work in the industry have to do all the juggling that other women—especially mothers—do, but magnified times ten because of the hours and the demands. I thanked the people who'd been there for me, especially my family. It's very hard not to cry when you talk about your family, and I had the whole place in tears. Then, to lighten the mood, I told the story about how even though my boys were fantastic and how being honoured here was a huge deal for me, I hadn't been able to persuade them to come.

"But when I told Josh he had a chance to lay Kim Cattrell, he changed his mind rather quickly," I told everyone.

The place exploded in laughter. I ended up getting a standing ovation. But it had come out completely wrong.

I meant to say "*meet* Kim Cattrell," of course. When I looked over at Josh, he had his head on the table. He's quite a proper kind of kid, and he was horrified. So was Hans. I don't think either of them spoke to me for a week.

When I was finished, I went and sat down at the head table. Kim came up to me when the awards had all been handed out. She has this incredibly husky voice, very sexy, sort of femme fatale. "I'd very much like to meet your son," she said with a wink.

We had a picture taken of the two of them together. She's gorgeous, dressed in this cinched black dress. Josh is standing there, his back straight as a board, his face flaming red.

On the very first day of school, parents hover in the school-yard, tears welling in their eyes as they try to part with their freshly scrubbed first grader. They mill around until the last backpack has disappeared into the building, then bravely head off to attempt to fill their day. Week by week, the mass of parents lingering by the door diminishes. And as kids move on to the higher grades, the number of eager mothers waiting in the schoolyard is, finally, nil. Some mums (or dads) may pull up to the curb with a squeal to let their kids leap into or out of the car, but those hours of hanging around are gone. Until, that is, the final years of high school. All of a sudden, those mums are back—and all of them are making an effort to be a Yummy Mummy. They stand around chatting as they wait, trying to sound interested in the gossip. But the truth is, all eyes are on the front gate. As dismissal time approaches, the mothers begin, almost involuntarily, to preen themselves. Hair is tossed, stomachs sucked in. Then the Grade 12 football team roars into the yard, and a hush descends on the waiting crowd. Gone are those awkward little-boy bodies. Calves and thighs now bulge through cloth-ing, shoulders are as wide as small sofas and a palpable wave of giddy flirtatiousness passes through the crowd of full-grown women as they watch the easy, back-slapping cama-raderie of these young men. But of course no mother can compete. Because also standing in the corner of the play-ground are their former selves, dressed to kill in low-slung jeans and tube tops: the next generation, the teenage girls.

– 8 –

Boys to men

I am a firm believer in orchestrating your life to make it as simple as possible. It gets complicated enough without my interference, so I'll have a shot at whatever I can do to smooth out the domestic chaos. My best move was to live across the road from the boys' school. That is, until girls came on the scene.

We'd decided early on that we wanted to make our home a hangout for our kids' friends. Parenting experts are always advising this so at least you know where they are and can keep an eye on what they're doing. Better in your house than a stranger's.

But as we entered the era of the big teens, our once-beautiful home began to look more like a mosh pit: bodies everywhere, sleeping or chatting among piles of litter—mostly pizza boxes and soda bottles. I bought myself a role of police tape—the kind you see blocking off the site of a murder—and taped crosses over doorways leading into my best rooms—our all-white living room, newly decorated bedroom and *our* bathroom. This approach had mixed results: the kids survived, the house not so much.

Then the female of the teen species began to arrive. Peering down into the basement packed with young girls dressed as if they were about to walk the streets of Paris on a hot summer's day, I asked Max why they didn't hang out at their own homes.

"They hate their mums," he told me. "They just don't understand them." (I can hardly believe young women are still using that line.)

Having been surrounded by testosterone for sixteen years, I rather liked the unfamiliar, girly vibe in our house. Floors coated in filthy running shoes the size of canoes now had a sprinkling of delicate, pastel sneakers. Coloured purses replaced hockey sticks as the accessory in our hallway. And the smell: sweetness mixed with sweat.

I was quite in awe of these sixteen- and seventeen-year-old girls. It's hard not to be aware of the energy and power of their amazing bodies as they strut around your house. These gorgeous young women should have been parading on the beaches of St. Tropez instead of lounging on piles of dirty boxers in the boys' rooms.

In fact, it was clear at the beginning of this new social adventure that the girls were far more mature than the boys. They would arrive looking as if they'd spent the entire day primping for the visit, and the guys would all be excited, flexing their muscles, playfully shoving one another (still dressed in their grubby PJs). Listening from upstairs, I could time it down to the second. The first twenty minutes were filled with giggles and hollers, music and mayhem. Then, suddenly, silence. The boys lost interest in the girls' gossip, and reverted to doing exactly what they'd been doing before—nothing. And the girls, bored with the knuckleheads in the basement, would come upstairs to perch around my kitchen table and chat with me about decorating (despite my having been banished minutes before).

Once, I was relaxing in the den after a busy day at work, eating Chinese food and enjoying a glass of wine when I heard a shriek. There was a girl at the doorway, hand over her mouth screaming. "Ohmigod! Did you know Debbie Travis is in your house?" Max just grunted. "She's my mum."

When the girls started chatting with me, the boys would complain. I could only tell them, "Well, look at the bunch of you. Hands in your crotch, talking about sports all the time. I wouldn't talk to you, either." They agonized nonstop about the hunt, but once they'd captured their prey, these young men had no idea what to do.

It was around that time the sleepovers began. Now, these were not the parent-orchestrated events of earlier years: a cute little child dropped off with blankey and teddy in tow. Not by a long shot. This was more refugee camp than romper room: a bunch of kids (male and female) sprawled all over, blankets and pillows everywhere. At first Hans and I would set our alarm every hour on the hour to make sure an orgy wasn't taking place under our roof. But we learned quickly that the whole process was incredibly benign, even kind of cute. They'd all just be sleeping, maybe cuddling a bit, boys and girls hanging out together. I liked to imagine it as a pyjama party, that they were playing Scrabble, maybe some charades (I know what you're thinking but I'm sticking with this vision). Still, it surprised me how rare it was to receive a call from one of the girls' parents, just to make sure we were home and that their daughters were safe. (I certainly would have called, remembering my own teen years snogging at the bus stop with the neighbourhood boys.)

But then slowly, over time, the sleepovers changed. The number of bodies decreased: at first it would be one of my boys, two of their male friends and one girl, until it was just one of my boys and a girl.

I finally had to accept that my vision of a pair of Scrabble-playing sons was out of date when I came home mid-afternoon and went up to one of the boys' rooms. Not thinking to knock (it was afternoon!), I burst in to find him and his girlfriend sitting in his bed, laptops out, the duvet pulled up around their chins, clearly very little on underneath. I didn't know what to do, what to say. All I could think of was our housekeeper going about her job on the floor below.

"You're going to scare Mary-Lou," I sputtered and staggered out.

For me, having relationships going on in the house (you've noticed I find it hard to say the S word) was a completely alien situation. It would never, *ever* have happened in my childhood home. I would not have risked even a quick snog with a boy in my parents' house.

My sisters were far more daring (maybe because they were younger and prettier—or so they claimed). Both of them had no fear.

As a teen, one of my sisters (I'm being deliberately vague here) had been rewarded for good behaviour with a small spare room downstairs that had its own side entrance. That way she could have some privacy when her friends came around (we don't have basements in England). This is how the story goes. My parents had left early one summer evening to go to the pictures. She was sixteen and supposed to be keeping an eye on the younger kids, but instead invited over Billy, her "boyfriend"—better known in the village as Bonking Billy.

My parents never made it to the movie. Instead, they bumped into some friends and decided to come back to our house to enjoy the lovely summer evening on our small patio—right outside her bedroom window. They mixed drinks and settled in, my mother chatting away about the small decorating venture she'd just tackled, turning the old spare room into a bedroom.

"What a wonderful idea!" her friend trilled.

"Oh, and I found the most chaaaarming Laura Ashley wallpaper!" my mother boasted. "You *must* take a look."

The four of them pressed their faces against the window and—let's just say that life was never quite the same in our house. Rules became much more rigid, and Mum rarely dropped her guard. As for chasing the local lads, from then on none of her daughters had a hope of sneaking them past our mother's eagle eye.

Looking back, I find it very funny, but for parents of girls especially, the introduction of sex into the parenting equation can be terrifying. Partly you worry about teen pregnancy (which is once again on the rise) and disease; partly you fret that your child isn't emotionally ready. But the other point is that kids' attitudes to sex and sexuality have changed dramatically, leaving parents reeling. The strangest trend (and I don't mean whether pastels are back this summer) is blow jobs in the back of the school bus. And the astonishing part is that the young women who are involved claim it's no big deal, that it makes them feel powerful and in control. Meanwhile, their shocked parents are scrambling, trying to figure out how to deal with this new attitude by attending seminars like "The Blow Job: Pros and Cons." Hard to believe, but if you don't go to such things, you're completely clueless. When I try to bring up the subject of sex with my sons, they head out of the room faster than you can say, well, blow job!

A couple of evenings ago, Josh asked us over dinner if we had ever heard of an amazing singer named Phil Collins.

"Are you kidding?" Hans said. "He's from our era!"

"Yeah, he has this incredible song called 'Sussudio.'"

"That was Our Song," I squealed in delight. "You were conceived to that song!"

Retching sounds filled the kitchen. "You are *so* disgusting, Mum. Thanks for ruining my life with that image!"

The truth is, much of what our children learn from us about intimacy and sexuality is not through a sit-down talk about the birds and the bees. They learn by watching us, and how we deal with our spouses—as they have since they were babies. It's our responsibility to show them how to treat their boyfriends or girlfriends with respect by what we do with our own life partners.

I've been lucky with Hans. When I come into a room, he still looks at me as if it's the first time we met. We've always been openly demonstrative with each other, and I have to admit he treats me like a queen—albeit an extremely annoying one. I think that the fact that our boys are comfortable being affectionate with their girlfriends is very much a result of them seeing us do the same.

The Drinking Dilemma

When I was a teenager, my mother was super-strict about drinking. She wouldn't know a joint if one walked in the house and introduced itself, but she could smell booze from the next county over. When I'd arrive home on the last bus from a night out at the local youth club, she would force me to breathe on her so she could check for any trace of alcohol. How humiliating is that? But I outsmarted her. She couldn't prove a thing after I'd licked away at a tube of toothpaste all the way home in the back of the bus.

My mother's strictness backfired with me. I thought nothing of swigging from bottles in her drinks' cabinet. My mum would tag her booze with pencil marks to track the contents, but I'd just dilute it with water. She figured out what was going on one afternoon when she was entertaining a group of girlfriends and poured them each a glass of sherry. I could see (and so could she) that the usually dark amber liquid looked more like pee. She had this way of slowly turning her head to glare at me that meant I was in deep trouble.

With my own boys, I took a rather different approach. We figured the better way to tackle the inevitable issues with teenagers and booze was to take the mystery out of drinking. We often had a bottle of wine at the dinner table and would offer them a splash, in the European style, where the waiters pour a small glass of wine for the children.

Still, we made it clear that this was something we only allowed at the family table. When the kids had their buddies over, it was another story. We'd learned from my friend with older children how careful parents need to be about what happens in their home.

One winter, when my friend's daughter was seventeen, she invited a group of girls that she'd met at camp—many of them from Florida—up to her family's country house. It was New Year's Eve, and her mother agreed that the girls could have one glass of champagne each at the local bar, which had been rented for a party. She and her husband would be outside exactly fifteen minutes past the stroke of midnight to take the girls home. But there always seems to be someone who spoils it for the whole gang. The girl in question drank all night, and by the time they were ready for pickup, she was passed out cold. My friend's husband spent the rest of the night in the country hospital while the girl had her stomach pumped. She was fine by morning—apart from a hangover she'll never forget.

The horror of this event was not that this young woman got so drunk (that happens), it was the following day when my friends were threatened with a lawsuit by the girl's parents. Not, *Thanks for looking after my daughter* or *Sorry she ruined your New Year's!* And even scarier than that, a lawsuit would not have been without legal precedent.

This was a huge lesson for us. Hans and I ended up taking all the booze out of our house for the next few years. I wasn't worried so much about my own children, but with all their friends hanging out at our place, the last drama we needed was for one of them to tuck into the whisky and fall down the stairs—or worse. The rule was that if they intended to have a drink, Hans would buy a case of beer, but they could only drink it hanging out in our basement or the backyard. We'd call the other parents and tell them our plan. If they disapproved of their kids joining in, that was fine, but at least they'd been given a choice and it was all aboveboard.

Talking to the other parents was key, because we'd discovered that as the boys hit their teens, different parenting styles became more and more obvious. Josh had one friend who has now become a legend in their school for his behaviour. As a parent you have an instinct about kids: there are the simply naughty ones, and then there are the ones you're truly nervous about. This boy was trouble. In any case, at the end of the term one year he invited a large group of buddies—including my boys—for a sleepover for the entire weekend. I called the boy's mother to check that she knew about the party and would be around. She assured me that both she and her husband would keep watch and that the kids had planned a wonderful weekend.

I had that niggling gut feeling that mothers experience, but the boys were excited and I finally agreed. In fact, Hans and I decided that since we had no kids for the weekend, we'd take advantage of an invitation to go to our own party at a cottage two hours out of the city. That evening, I stood with a glass of wine gazing out over a pristine lake. The patio was packed, and I scanned the crowd to see whom I knew. Standing there in the middle of a large group were the parents of the child whose house my kids were probably going wild in!

I weaved my way through the throng and spoke to the mother. "I thought you were going to be home," I said.

"Oh, they'll be fine!" she told me dismissively.

I would probably have agreed and stayed to enjoy the evening, but Hans glared at me and said we were going home. *Great*, I thought, *another two hours down the highway!*

We drove straight to the family's house. There were kids everywhere, a strong smell of pot in the air, police cruisers and even an ambulance out front. Apparently someone had tumbled off a trampoline while intoxicated and suffered a couple of broken limbs. The police had arrested the host of the party, and my kids were nowhere to be found.

Our next stop was our house. There, to our relief, were six boys, including our own two, watching a movie in the basement. They had seen the trouble brewing and had left the party early. This time I forgave the pizza boxes spread all over the floor, ruffled their hair and went up to bed.

I don't mean to sound as if my kids are perfect. They're not, and I certainly have an inkling of the kinds of antics they've got up to over the years. (If the goldfish bowl is anything to go by, they've certainly had their moments—on more than one occasion I've come down to find it used as a receptacle for throwing up.) But part of growing up is keeping things from your parents until you're *all* old enough to laugh about it. (I'm not there yet!)

To me—and I know this is a personal subject—illegal drugs are a different story. The stakes are so much higher if anything goes wrong. Whether or not to tell your teenagers about your own drug experiences (if any) has become a debate among my friends. The kids are definitely going to ask. My approach has been to deny everything—in a muffled kind of way—"Nah, makes me cough, and your dad passes out if he even sees a needle."

I've also used another diversionary tactic. The first time they asked Hans and me if we'd ever smoked pot, I said, "If you want to know that, I'll have to tell you about our sex life, too." That stopped the questions cold.

The problem is, if you tell your children you've tried drugs, it gives them the luxury of turning the tables and saying, "Well, you did it, so why shouldn't I?" You do not want to have this conversation in the emergency room. I had a friend die from a speed overdose when I was a teenager, and I've never lost the fear factor.

I'm not saying my boys haven't tried. They probably have, but I've never heard about it. I actually think it's just fine that it's never come out. It means they didn't screw up so badly that I had to bail them out. They respected my disapproval enough that they didn't want to mess with me.

Driving Lessons

When you're the mother of a toddler, your greatest fear is about when she'll tumble down the stairs or if she'll knock her head on the glass coffee table. It seems scary at the time, but it's nothing compared with worrying about your teenager. When kids are young, parents are actually in control: you can act as bodyguard on the stairs and simply move the table to a safer place. But once they hit the teen years they are making their own decisions. You still love them the way you did when they were little and you got a lump in your throat snuggling them when they were all sweet and clean after bath time. But once they tower over you, the lump in the throat comes from a heady mixture of pure love and pure *please-let-them-come-home-in-one-piece* terror.

There are three main parental fears at this age: drinking,

drugs and driving. Driving is probably the most frightening (and a fatal cocktail when combined with any of the others). Even if you decide your children won't get behind the wheel until they're twenty (and I know people who've come to this agreement with their kids—albeit with bribery involved), it doesn't matter. They are going to spend time in their friends' vehicles. The car is the beginning of freedom for many teens, and to drive for the first time is giddy stuff. For me, the feeling of no longer having to rely on our village bus (which only came every few hours) was paradise. It was like growing wings.

When I was living in London in my late teens and early twenties, I drove a little French Citroën that resembled a fat, green frog. The engine had no more power than a Singer sewing machine, and I had a tough time driving up steep hills—except in reverse. But I loved that car because it gave me the freedom to take off when I wanted. If I had a date with some guy who turned out to be a creep, I could always make a quick getaway in my car.

At eighteen, I worked on a photo shoot with four other girls at the stunning country house of a very famous British photographer. The place was a mansion, and we all ending up sleeping in the various bedrooms—not a particularly bright idea since the old git's wife was away. The first night, he tried his luck crawling into bed with each one of us. Every time he was rejected, he just moved on to the next. He finally gave up and returned to his room, but the four of us weren't sure how long he'd stay there. Once again, that faithful Citroën came to my rescue: we all piled in and made our escape.

There are some things that have changed, of course, since I passed my driver's licence—mostly for the better. My children would never consider *not* buckling up. They still scold me relentlessly to put on my seat belt. The same goes for drinking and driving: today's kids have had the horrors of driving under the influence drilled into them. It's a far cry from when I was a teenager. My friend Carolynne remembers that when she was a girl, her father would turn to her in the back seat of the family car and ask her to pour him a glass of Scotch!

I have had my fair share of near misses in the car (okay, on a daily basis). My kids like to tell anyone who'll listen that I'm the worst driver in the world. Sure, there was the cow I hit when I was taking my driving test at seventeen. The beast wobbled off, but the driving instructor threw me out and left me on the side of the road! And that, of course, was nothing compared with the incident an hour before our wedding.

My mother had sent me to the farmer's wife up the road to have my hair done. I came out looking like Shirley Temple, with all these really tight ringlets. I was in a wee panic as I drove our rented car back to my parents' house, looking in the mirror and tugging at the curly springs. Suddenly I saw the milkman's small truck hurtling toward me. I swerved, but to the wrong side, and it was too late. I hit him straight on. I was fine, but the milkman looked the worse for wear (he ended up with a broken collarbone and a fear of female drivers for the rest of his life).

We were in the deepest countryside without a cellphone, and I knew I had to act fast. I leapt over the stone wall and legged it through the field into the kitchen of a local farmer. There, sitting around an old pine table, was the quintessential rosy-cheeked English farm family: Mum, Dad and three robust-looking children. Each one had a soup spoon frozen in mid-air as I barged in.

"Hi, you might not remember me. I'm Debbie Travis but I used to be Debbie Short and my mother is Valerie—you know, the one who used to take in lodgers? I helped with the harvest, oh, fifteen years ago? Anyway, I'm getting married at Whalley Abbey in about an hour and my hair is a terrible fright. Oh, and I have just had a car crash. Do you think I could call my mother?"

They just sat staring at me as if I was insane, and pointed to their phone. By the time I'd run back across the field, there was a lineup of cars. All the guests who were invited to the wedding had started to arrive, and they were stuck behind the accident site in a great, winding queue that went all the way to the next village.

My mother was outside the church talking to Hans, dressed like a movie star in his morning coat. When she spotted me leaping over the wall, she tried frantically to cover his eyes, since it is always bad luck for the groom to look at the bride before the wedding.

It was all completely absurd, but it also broke the ice, in a way. Everyone met everyone else out there on the road. The police ended up coming to the wedding and partied with all the models. A good time was had by all—and a precedent was set for all the calamities, chaos and hilarity that would follow in our life together.

But that, of course, was more than twenty years ago. I'm not as bad a driver as my children would have people believe. And, anyway, there is nothing worse than being criticized by a bunch of lazy teenagers whom *you* are chauffeuring around.

Both boys took summer jobs after they passed their driving tests. They broke their backs landscaping for three months, but at the end pooled their savings and bought themselves a second-hand runaround. It now sits in my driveway like a rusty old bean can.

It may be my British upbringing, but I find nothing more obnoxious than seeing a seventeen-year-old cruising the streets in a luxury car. It's actually quite sad, because it leaves them so little to look forward to, like that deep pleasure of purchasing a special car (or some other extravagance) with money they've actually earned. Of all the vehicles I've had over the years, it's those first old clunkers that hold the happiest memories.

School's Out

For both teenagers and their parents, high-school graduation is a stew of mixed feelings. You're elated that your child is finished, that your role in their education is largely over, but it can also be tough—even sad—to say farewell to your favourite teachers and a place that has become a major part of family life. Through the tears, you choose to forget the many Saturday-morning detentions, the horrendous school trips and favouritism at prize giving. You push to the back of your mind parent-teacher night with your adult-sized bum squeezed into a miniature chair, knees poking you in the face while you look up into the hairy nostrils of the French teacher explaining (nastily) that you should not be looking at a future in languages for your child. You obliterate the memory of the countless afternoons the principal called you in for "a few words" in his office.

But I went even further. I also forgot Lasagna Day and my vow to leave the school organizing to other mothers. At graduation I became my nemesis: the Volunteer Vulture.

Josh was the first to graduate, and I was as excited as the next parent. As we forty mothers and one or two fathers sat in the school gymnasium, the teachers explained what we were in for. It was not simply a cap and gown ceremony—no way!—it involved barbecues, sleepovers and fancy balls, cocktail parties for the parents and families.

When it came time to assign responsibility for the cocktail portion of the festivities, I must have had a brain surge or something, because I was practically out of my seat, waving my arm more wildly than any of the usual suspects. There was silence in the room as the English teacher who'd been in charge of grad for the past twenty years looked at me with a mixture of pity and glee. She knew full well that I hadn't done my share of volunteering over the years. Payback time was written all over her face.

In that moment, however, I was oblivious. I was so caught up in the excitement of graduation. I wish someone had told me the sort of insanity it incites in the various playground species. The Yummy Mummy goes wild: a little nip and tuck, outfits that would better suit a royal wedding. The Domestic Diva has events planned for the kids that would put the Olympic organizing committee to shame. And at every meeting, for every event, the Volunteer Vulture nearly dislocates her shoulder waving frantically, offering to take on more—MORE!

It wasn't long before I realized that the pre-grad party I'd signed up for was going to be a huge job. I'd been thinking hot dogs in the driveway, but I was told, "Oh, no, Ms. T., the Bloomberrys hosted last year's grad, and they hired a full orchestra!" Then I tried to weasel out of it, but they wouldn't release me from my duties. The worse part was that the hostess was expected to foot the bill!

Not anymore. I put together a committee of mums, and eventually, after endless meetings, we pooled some money and recruited as host one of the parents who owned an Indian restaurant. By that time, I'd been demoted to head of the decorating committee. I started off with a group of twenty mothers. We met every Wednesday, Thursday and Saturday morning to discuss the colour of the flowers for the tables. "Choose a fucking colour," I believe I said at one point. "Ms. T said the F word," someone whispered loudly enough for everyone to hear.

Then we held weeks of committee meetings on where the coats should be put (desperate, I voted for a breakout group to discuss this matter but was shot down), moving on to the length of the sheers used to create ambience and hide the huge stainless steel buffet—an eyesore in my brilliant design plan. There were endless arguments about every single decision, no matter how minor. Used to running this kind of project in my sleep, I lost all patience. Tempers had reached the heat of a Madras curry when, one evening, several of the mothers walked out.

The next day I received an eleven-page letter of resignation from one of the committee members. She said that this was a school project, not a Debbie Travis one. I came home crying.

I didn't want Josh to know what was going on. I wanted him to be thrilled that his mum had orchestrated a beautiful graduation cocktail party. I wanted him to be proud of me and of himself—the boy who had failed sandboxing. So I kept on going. By the day of graduation, we were down to six committee members. We set up the restaurant with swaths of billowing sari fabric, little potted flowers all around the walls. Someone helping out complained that she didn't like the turquoise fabric, and that it looked cheap because it was nylon. I had to stop myself from blowing a gasket. *It was free!* I wanted to shout. *It's in candlelight!*

Someone else freaked out because there were four homeless guys who always sat outside the restaurant. Easy, I said, and gave them each fifty bucks to spend the evening around the corner. The red carpet I'd ordered for the pavement outside turned out to be black, and one Yummy Mummy's hair caught fire on the torches I'd rented, but in the end the party was a big success, the restaurant looked spectacular and the kids and their families all had a wonderful time.

The following morning I received a call from a mother who'd arrived early to help clean up. I was also headed over to take down the fabric and remove the potted plants. But she told me that there was nothing left. One of the waiters explained that all these women in Mercedeses had pulled up seconds after the graduation was finished that night and walked out with armloads of plants and all the fabric. They'd taken everything. There was not a petal left.

The graduation ceremony itself was lovely. My whole family, including my stepfather and his wife, Elizabeth, had all come for the event. The entire group was dressed to the nines. Everyone, that is, except Josh. As we crossed the road to the school, I watched him, completely appalled: his shoes had the backs all broken down, his suit was shiny in the elbows and knees and his collar was frayed.

"Look at you! You're in tatters!" I said, grabbing the collar of his favourite shirt, the one he'd been wearing for years. The whole thing ripped right off in my hand, pulling the front of the shirt with it. Gobsmacked for a second, we then roared with laughter. Whatever. He went up and was awarded his graduation prize looking like a tramp.

Sitting there beside Max, still a year away from his own moment but so close that we could all nearly taste it, I watched Josh, my eyes brimming with tears. Proud of him, proud of his brother, and proud of us. We'd made it.

Motherhood and guilt will forever be entwined. Ivy wrapped around a tree. Impossible to tell where one begins and the other ends. But we have to ask, Can they be untangled? Can we throw off the guilt? Even a vine or two?

There are many theories circulating these days about how it is that our kids turn out the way they do. One suggests that parents mould their children from the day they're born, shaping them into the sort of person they'd like them to be. If things go wrong, and your child becomes a difficult teen or fails to get a scholarship to Harvard, it's all your fault—and the guilt sticks like glue. Another theory is that kids come into the world with their own unique personalities, strengths and weaknesses, abilities and challenges, and all we have to do as parents is nourish that child into greatness. Odds are, though, that they won't become the "superkid" you envisioned, so you must have screwed up somewhere along the way—again, a recipe for guilt.

But the truth—as any parent who's made it across the finish line will tell you—is that the way your child turns out is some mysterious mixture of sorcery, nature, nurture and hard, hard work. We can't spend all our time and energy blaming ourselves for our children's shortfalls—or slapping ourselves on the back for their successes!—because in the end they become their own person and we love them regardless. The mystery of how they got there and what role we played in it is part of the joy of the journey.

The kids are all right

When I left home at seventeen, it didn't seem as if I was too young—not to me or my parents. Most kids I knew were setting out on their own, getting their own place, learning a trade. Not many were headed off to college—in the working-class north of England, few of my classmates had the opportunity, and it wasn't something that was widely encouraged anyway. Going to university just didn't seem as crucial then as it does today—I was never made to feel as if I was unemployable because I lacked a degree.

In fact, I was thrilled to leave behind the confines of village life and do things my own way. I figured I was ready to take on the world. When I went off to Milan on that first modelling job, I barely consulted my mother, I just up and left.

The minute I was back on British soil, I headed straight for London. I arrived at the famous Victoria Station like a public service ad for *What Not to Do: Teenage Girl Edition,* suitcases at my feet, a lost look on my face. I sat down in a coffee shop and scoured the For Rent section of the *London Evening Standard.* I quickly realized that there was no way I could afford a place on my own, so I set off to visit addresses listed in the Flatmate Wanted column.

There is nothing weirder than sitting in a strange, tiny room being drilled with questions by kids not much older than you to see if you'll fit in with their lifestyle and do your fair share of the cleaning. It definitely makes a girl feel a long way from home! As luck would have it, though, I landed a spot with two other girls in the third hovel I viewed. One was a wacko, but the other became a firm friend. Within the month we had enough courage to split and find our own place.

Linda was a Page 3 Girl—which meant she had a killer body and gigantic boobs, so would always be cast in the sexy modelling jobs, including the famous topless shot on page 3 of *The Sun* newspaper. These models were treated like royalty by every bloke in England. (I was doing mostly catalogues and teen magazines—quite a bore in comparison.)

Linda and I found a place just off Sloane Square in the heart of London's Chelsea area (thanks to my glamour granny, who knew the owner). The four-storey Victorian mansion was a rabbit warren of rooms, but it was strangely empty except for an old man named Dicky who looked after the place and lived on the second floor.

When we first walked in, we were completely spooked. Dark and dingy, it was decorated with thick red pile carpet, stuffed birds and oversized gilt frames depicting a series of mad-looking aristocrats. It was like something out of a horror film.

Dicky was mesmerized by Linda's breasts, and the place was ours. He gave us the basement. It was actually just one large living room, plus a sad-looking kitchen and tiny bathroom. Linda set up her bed in the living area, and I took the broom closet under the stairs. I could slot in a single mattress and some shelves. We loved that place.

We had very little money, since we'd just started out in the modelling world. We even took waitressing jobs to help buy clothes—being poor was no excuse for not being glam. We'd go hang out in wine bars and have some guys take us out for big dinners, then ditch them—head out the back door, RUN!—before they could ask for more.

We were so busy partying that we didn't notice that we hadn't seen Dicky for a while. No one else was living in the house and we'd come home at all hours. But then this horrible smell started getting stronger and stronger. Finally, we went upstairs and found that poor old Dicky had been dead for several days.

After that, a Saudi millionaire bought the house, and for an entire year we avoided paying rent. When they finally decided to make the place into a hotel, as sitting tenants we confidently had them buy us out. Linda and I had agreed we'd settle for £300 a person. On the phone with the lawyer I explained, "We'll accept three each." He said, "All right, £3,000 each it is."

We were flabbergasted. That was a fortune in those days, and I still have every penny of that money in a low-interest account back in England. I thought of it as my back-door money, my security.

I'm not sure what my mother made of it all. She was probably a bit apprehensive when I left home, but she never interfered—not exactly the route I took when Josh headed off to university in London. First of all, I went with him. We flew to England together, and arrived groggy the next morning at his King's College dormitory. Weighed down with suitcases, boxes of war books and sports equipment, the two of us nervously "checked in." The boy behind the desk, who didn't look a day over nine, winked at me as he handed us a key and directions to Josh's room. The smell in the elevator was overwhelming, a distinct potpourri of urine and sweat. Josh didn't seem to notice. We found his room easily, since it was straight across from the elevator.

"Oh dear," I said. "This could be pretty noisy."

"It's fiiiiine, Mum. Easier for me to find my room at four in the morning," he said.

We opened the door and I stepped back, mostly because it was nearly impossible to both fit in the room. The place was more cupboard than anything else. Yes, you may be thinking, but *you* lived in a closet under the stairs when you were that age! The difference was that mine had only ever been inhabited by a mop and bucket. This "room" had the scars of hundreds of students who'd parked themselves there over the years. There was a cracked sink, a hook and a couple of hangers, plus a narrow desk and a cot attached to the wall. My name is Debbie Travis, and I have made over more desperate spaces than most people have had hot dinners, but this time even I was speechless. Of course it could have been the hairball I'd just inhaled that was lodged in the back of my throat.

My precious boy clapped his hands in happiness. "Pretty amazing, Mum!" he said.

I looked around, wondering for a moment if I'd been mistaken and we were actually in the coat closet of his new suite.

"Look, there's a note for you," Josh said, handing me a one-page printout.

Good, I thought, *this will explain everything!*

"Dear mother of the student standing next to you," I read, looking over at Josh with a smile. "We welcome you to King's College London. Sadly, we know how you are feeling at this precise moment, but do not bother to come back down to reception. This is where your child will live for his first year. If it makes you feel any better, all the rooms are just as gross. . . ."

"Well!" I huffed, as I headed out to buy some highly toxic chemicals to disinfect the nightmare room, passing the smirking midget at reception who'd obviously witnessed this reaction countless times that day.

When I returned, I brought back my best friend, Jacky, whom I've known since we were in our early twenties. Wearing elbow-length rubber gloves, wellington boots and masks, we attacked the room full force. Every so often we'd head out into the hallway for air and would be greeted by mothers from around the globe, wearing desperate smiles and similar cleaning gear. I did my best, but when it came to getting down on my hands and knees on the stinky, crispy industrial carpet, I begged Jacky for help. My brave friend held her nose and gave it a shot. Halfway in, she couldn't bear it any longer. "I love you and I love Josh," she said. "But scrubbing some other student's semen out of the carpet is pushing our friendship too far!"

Wherever our kids go, whatever they do, parents never truly cut the umbilical cord. Even when they're on the other side of the world (especially when they're on the other side of the world), your children remain a priority in your thoughts and in your life—it's not something you shake off like a pesky fly. When my mum died, her mother was still healthy and well. She lived to be nearly ninety, working in her antique store right until the end. But she never mentioned my mother's name again. It was far too painful for her.

My friend Kit—who's a mother of three and my business partner in our TV production company—has been through a lot with me. We've watched each other's children grow up and leave the house, we've shared success and rejection in our work. There have been many days we've spent calling each other back and forth while we wait and wait to hear if we've been awarded the green light to film or if a certain show has been renewed. I always know it's bad news when the first thing she announces when she calls me is, "The kids are fine."

Of course, we're utterly destroyed when something we've worked for doesn't pan out, but it reminds us of our priorities. Our children aren't on crack and haven't been in a car crash, so things can't be that bad. It brings us back to what is really important and why it is we're living the crazy, busy lives we are: for ourselves and our families and to have an interesting life. If the kids are all right, everything is going to be okay in the end.

The Missing Stitch

Mothers today have so much to learn from the women of my mum's generation. They were so tough. Their job was to put food on the table, look after their children and appear respectable for the neighbours—all of which they achieved with a single-minded determination and, I think, without anywhere near the level of guilt. They just did what they had to do to make their lives work. They hadn't the time to create the sort of problems that plague so many mums now—struggling to shrink back to their pre-child figure in record time, lunging and squatting, using their stroller as a support bar; fighting to get their genius child into a supernursery. This kind of stuff never occurred to women like my mum because they were too busy simply surviving.

I never understood my mother's life at all when I was a child. I just craved a piece of her attention and for her to be proud of me. Later I promised myself that when I was a mother I'd be different. I'd never be bad-tempered or impatient with my children. I would be the perfect mother.

But being a parent is nothing if not an extreme lesson in humility—everything you swore you would never do, you do. In fact, I am probably a lot more like my mother than even I realize. I hope so. I will always feel sad that because she died before my children were born, I missed the chance to ask her about motherhood, about her own hopes and dreams. I often imagine how different our lives would be if she was there for me and my sisters and brother to chat with about our own family dramas. I regret those awkward teenage years when I wasted so much energy arguing with her about every damn thing, then spending my twenties utterly self-absorbed. I wish I'd had more time with her. "Be nice to me—I could be dead tomorrow!" I often tell my own kids. Shameful, I know, but you have to use every weapon you have!

And yet, the world is different now. My mother couldn't have imagined the kind of life that I lead, balancing a busy international career and family, working with my husband, juggling three large offices in two cities and many employees. Mothers today are determined to have it all. It's hardly a burden—we have to be thankful to the women who broke ground for us and made it possible—but because the terrain is new, we're still struggling to sort out the balance.

This is the missing stitch for so many of us. We have the solid, honest example of the mothers who came before us—at least in their easygoing attitude toward their kids—but we have to forge our own way, as well. We're charting new ground, and we can't expect our lives and our families to be flawless. Except for rare moments, life will never behave as you expect it to behave. And that's all right. It's the crazy, manic, wacky stuff that happens in our lives as mothers that we can laugh most about, that we can sit around and share with our friends—even our grown-up kids.

Of course, when you're the mother of young children, having an empty nest (or sitting around enjoying the company of your adult children) seems like something that happens in some other universe. Just the thought of heading out to a movie without the bother of finding a babysitter—let alone having the house all to yourself—is pure luxury.

A journalist once asked me (she must have been a single-ton) if I was ever lonely when I travelled on business. "Lonely? You must be kidding!" I hooted. "It's pure heaven to walk into a strange hotel room, soak in a hot bubble bath with a glass of wine, surrounded by silence—no one calling my name, no action figure stuck between my buttocks, no husband about to pounce on my exhausted bones!"

But you feel different about all of it when your children have actually flown the coop. It's like embarking on a diet: when certain foods are banned, they become even more tantalizing; once you're off the diet you don't crave them half so much. It's the same when your kids leave home. All the freedom you dreamed about over the years is now there for the asking, but instead of liberated you feel oddly empty. The house is eerily quiet and way too tidy. The Lego has long been packed away with all their favourite toys and the boxes of yellowing schoolwork.

I'm at a point in my career when jobs are abundant—hosting this or that TV series, public-speaking engagements in exotic countries and countless business opportunities. You can now buy a Debbie Travis home, Debbie Travis paint and products for your house, watch my shows, read my books and newspaper columns. It's thrilling and exactly what I've worked hard for twenty years to achieve. If I'd had some of these offers ten years ago, I simply wouldn't have been able to accept them because I had kids at home. But now that I have the freedom to grab opportunities in far-off places I wonder if I really want them. Maybe I should just enjoy the spot I've gotten to, kick back and relax. . . .

Nah, not just yet! I am one of the lucky ones. My career has been a source of enormous pleasure in my life and will continue to be for a long time. It's the people who have neglected themselves and their own needs who feel most lost when their children leave home.

It's one of the reasons it's so important to pay attention to what makes *you* happy, to stretch yourself even while you're raising kids: cultivate that green thumb, take a course in graphic design, hike those mountains in Peru or throw yourself into a career you love. Because when they're gone, it's your opportunity to really indulge those passions, including the one that has been at the very bottom of the pecking order for the last two decades: your partner.

The pattern in your relationship changes the minute the pushing begins in the birthing room. It seems as if you've been transformed in the blink of an eye from a flirtatious singleton—confident and beautiful, the man of your dreams on your arm—into a shrew with a tongue that would put a drunken sailor to shame. The minute you return to the nest, the game of fetch begins. *Get me some diapers. Pick up some milk. Don't forget to feed the dog.* It doesn't stop until the last child leaves home.

In our household, Hans has been quite happy doing as he's told and taking a back seat. Stirring my cuppa tea one morning not long ago, I complained to Max, who was munching a piece of toast before heading off to college. "I worry about him, he seems thinner and less active. He's looking old. Maybe he should have a visit to a specialist."

"I hadn't noticed." Max said. "Dad looks fine to me."

"God, not your father!" I said, waving the thought away. "The goldfish."

It's easy to forget about them when you're busy maintaining the delicate balance of family, work and friends.

And men so often fall into the trap of waiting for their wife's lead in everything they do. I often wonder why they allow themselves to be bossed around in this way. After all, they're grown men and far from pushovers at work. I figure it's partly love, and partly the path of least resistance. They just want the status quo. For most guys, "Just tell me what to do and what to buy and I'm on it" is now part of their DNA. Smile, run and fetch.

I have trained Hans well over the years and he generally does all his chores without complaint, but occasionally he still slips up. Now, this is a clever guy who runs several companies and has a staff that is 80 per cent female—you would think he'd learned a thing or two over the years—but Mother's Day and my birthday are a guaranteed disaster in our house.

More often than not, I wait upstairs in tears listening to him in a last-minute panic, waking up the teenagers to go get croissants while he makes the usual card with an IOU. (I have a shoebox full of those!) All other celebrations are happy times in our home—Christmas, kids' birthdays, his birthday—because *I* organize them.

When I actually do receive a present, I have learned to use the tools of a Method actor to avoid revealing my true feelings as I unwrap the garden hose or a nightie a granny wouldn't be caught dead in. But the worst—the very worst—was last summer.

My birthday is at the end of June, which means we can have the cake and cards (the ones I bought!) in the garden.

Last summer, we had our whole family and a couple of neighbours and friends around for a celebratory drink. I was surprised and delighted to see a great big parcel the size of a large cake box sitting on the table with a card from Hans.

I saved it until last. With the coyness of a teenage girl I began to remove the wrapping from my beloved's gift, all memories of previous fiascos wiped clear. The small crowd looked on. But as the box was revealed, there was a gasp.

"Oh dear," said Helen from next door.

"Daaaad!" Josh said, looking aghast at his father.

Several guests began to back away, fear in their eyes. I ripped off the remaining paper and stared at the box—speechless. It was a bathroom scale.

"It's the latest super-duper digital model. It's really accurate!" Hans beamed, completely clueless.

"I'm going to bed now," I gulped.

Men don't really mean any harm—unlike women, they don't lash out like that on purpose. And after all, if you're lucky, he's still there beside you—even though he's been on the back burner amid all the noise of your growing family. For the past two decades, you've been too tired when you crawl into bed to even talk (never mind anything else). You've perfected the Look for the kids, as well as the one you reserve especially for him. The first poke in the back and "Hi there, sexy," and you can give that Look without even turning around—the one that has him scurrying to the other side of the bed. Well, now it's payback time. He may not be quite as cute anymore—but, I'm afraid, neither are you! That guy needs a big, big hug and an enormous amount of attention. In our case, Hans bought a motorbike instead.

As they've left home, our boys have also developed a new kind of relationship with their dad. Respect came out of the trauma of the teens, and now that friendship is solid: man to man. With Max and Josh both away at university, it's Hans whom they call daily. *I* am now taking the back burner—which is just fine.

Last summer, when they were both home for a few weeks, they pulled in to our place in the middle of the night with a pack of friends making such a racket that they must have woken up the entire neighbourhood. Eventually I stormed downstairs in my pyjamas, hair sticking out in every direction. I walked into the kitchen and saw my kids and their friends lined up at the counter doing tequila shots. They were laughing and hooting and hollering.

"You better stop this right now!" I said, searching my mental database for a reason that didn't make me look even more uncool. "You're . . . you're going to wake up your father!"

"Uh, Ms. T?" one of the boys' friends said, pointing behind me to the kitchen table. There was Hans, shot glass to his lips, looking sheepish.

It may not seem like every mother's proudest moment—beloved husband knocking back tequila with the kids—but I look at the big picture. When you first stare into the eyes of your newborn child, you're engulfed in the moment, and you know in your deepest core that you will never love anyone as much as this. You're not dreaming about your daughter becoming a corporate lawyer or a beauty queen or your son at the head of the World Bank or trotting onto the field as a football hero. It's not about award-winning grades or sports medals. If you could make a wish at that moment it would be that your family will be healthy and happy and remain together. Nothing more, nothing less. And that's what I saw looking around my beaten-up kitchen table, years of memories carved into its old wooden surface: young gentlemen, comfortable in their own skin, hanging out with good friends and having fun with their parents—albeit one of them unshaven in a scruffy bathrobe with a brimming glassful of tequila.

My Ten Commandments

1. Treat your kids like a paint job. It's all in the preparation. Take the time to sand and prime well and the results will be as good as perfect. Don't worry too much about the cracks or blotches—they just add character.

2. Make life as easy as possible. Do not be afraid to cut corners.

3. Learn to use the word *no* at every opportunity. Your children will soon get bored and move on to the next demand.

4. Burn your child-rearing books. Or stack them up and stand on them so you can reach your towering teen to be able to shout at him eye to eye. Or build a wall with them to separate bickering siblings. Or use them to swipe a naughty kid on the bum as they run for cover.

5. Be prepared for war. You need a brilliant strategy and state-of-the-art weapons to raise a family. Conquer your children early on but be forewarned, they are masters of the element of surprise.

for Feeling No Guilt

6. Don't be afraid to ask for help. When the going gets tough, call for real-life backup. Share your failures with other leaders as they may have more advanced weaponry up their sleeve.

7. A good tantrum clears the air. I'm talking about you here: learn from your kids that crying can get you what you want.

8. Follow your kids' lead in laughter, games and plain silliness. They know best about some things.

9. Love the chaos. Praise your messy house daily, even pray to it, because before you blink, your children will be gone and it will be way too tidy.

10. Look after yourself. The wheels on the bus go round and round . . . and round and round. Learn to take a break. Never be ashamed to tell the family you're leaving, and you're going alone, even if its only for twenty-four hours. They will survive.

Dear Mum,

When you told us you were writing this book we were a
bit surprised. In all honesty, at first we weren't quite sure
what qualified you to write about parenting. Our memories of our childhood are marked by rather hectic and
crazy times. You always seemed to be setting the kitchen
on fire, delivering us late to games and practices (if you
even remembered where we were playing) and you often
forgot our friends' names—and really nothing has changed!

But, Mum, none of that matters. We grew up in our
own way and became athletes and intelligent young men.
No matter how busy you were, you managed to blow us
away with home-cooked meals that we loved, even if the
local fire department was "invited" as well. You were always
unique, and many of our friends adore you, and our closest ones still call you "Mum" too!

When we were still in grade school, we would often

watch you from our classroom windows as you loaded up the jeep with ladders and paint. Even then, we knew you were different—especially as our teachers would nag us to put a good word in to get you to come and do their homes. We know you as someone who is always busy, always on the go doing this and that, but through it all you have always been there for us.

You prepared us for the world by making us learn from our mistakes and giving us endless hugs. You made us who we are. A good parent is not defined by their perfection, but rather by their imperfections. So, Mum, never feel guilty for not always getting it right and often losing it—we love you anyway.

– Your naughty boys, Josh and Max

Acknowledgements

This book could not have been written without the hourly support of my publisher, Anne Collins, who screamed with laughter at every story whether she really found it hilarious or not. She mothered me every step of the way.

As you may have guessed, I love to tell a funny tale—but putting it down on paper is a challenge. I am indebted to Andrea Curtis, who worked alongside me at all hours on getting this book right at the same time as she was juggling the demands of her own young family.

I would particularly like to thank Cathy Paine who has been my publicist and great friend for many years. She jumped at the idea of me writing a parenting book, even though it is a far cry from anything I have ever done.

My gratitude goes out to the whole Random House Canada team: Pamela Murray, the managing editor, who kept track of all the bits; Alison Reid, the copy editor, who identified all my dangling participles; creative director Scott Richardson for his patience while designing a book jacket for the "queen of colour"; Kylie Barker, who spent far too much time going through my family photos. Thanks also to Jennifer Shepherd and Samantha North for dealing with the contract so speedily, and to Jennifer and Ron Eckel for taking on the job of selling the rights to my book around the world.

My hugs and kisses (yes, I'll buy the next round of drinks) to my friends Jacky, Jennifer, Ruth and Danielle, who have shared their mummy moments with hilarity and honesty. And of course to Helen, my Irish friend. I am so fortunate you live next door. As both a mother and a doctor, you helped me with the research. "Well, you'd better get your facts right," you said, and then gave me even more of your valuable time. I am forever in your debt.

My parents made me what I am today, and I am completely grateful for that. I am also grateful to my stepfather, John, to my brother, Will, and my sisters Joanna and Emma who have given me the strength to put our childhood down on paper.

Most of all I salute my family, whom I have used shamelessly in order to tell these stories. My two precious sons, Josh and Max; who I hounded for every family tale even when they were writing exams. If you fail college, I will forgive you both. My husband, Hans, listened patiently as I read every chapter out loud to him, over and over again. He is the love of my life.

DEBBIE TRAVIS is the author of eight bestselling books and an internationally syndicated newspaper column. She has produced and hosted three highly successfully television series, including *Debbie Travis's The Painted House*, *Debbie Travis's Facelift* and *From the Ground Up*. Her paint and home product line, The Debbie Travis Collection, is sold coast to coast. She lives in Montreal with her family.